# PAWS
# &JAWS

# PAWS &JAWS

## DR RADHA VASAN

PARTRIDGE

A Penguin Random House Company

**To order additional copies of this book, contact**
Partridge India
000 800 10062 62
orders.india@partridgepublishing.com

www.partridgepublishing.com/india

# Acknowledgements

This book is dedicated to Lizzy, my boxer, who gave a new lease to my boring life! She does not think she is a dog but a part of the human race!

I owe my creativity and imagination to my 2 sons, who encouraged and believed that if anybody could write a book in our family, I could! They stood by me through all my impatience, my short-fuse, and my obsession to finish the book early! I am grateful to them for very helpful and insightful inputs and reactions to various passages in the book.

To my husband, I say, thanks partner, for your tolerance and wisdom.

My parents are my backbone, who instilled the love of books in me and encouraged the art of story-telling from early childhood. To my father especially, who is always proud of his daughter in any wild venture she undertakes! A loving dad, who is my dartboard for bouncing ideas off and giving valuable advice.

I also wish to express my appreciation to the many people who stood by my whacky ideas and always encouraged me and believed I would succeed. Here's to you, Dr. Punam, Dr. Annie and my staff in VR department of my hospital.

# (1)

The greatest love is a mother's; then a dog's; then a sweetheart's. → Polish proverb.

**A** dog's prayer . . . .

*Dear GOD,*

*When we get to heaven, can we sit on your couch? Or is it the same old story?*

*Why are there cars named after the Jaguar, the Cougar, the Mustang, the Colt, the Stingray, and the Rabbit, but not ONE is named for a dog? How often do you see a cougar riding around? We dogs love a nice ride! Would it be that hard to rename the Chrysler Eagle, the Chrysler Beagle?*

*If a dog barks his head off in the forest, and no human hears him, is he still a bad dog?*

*We dogs can understand human verbal instructions, hand signals, whistles, horns, clickers, beepers, scent ID's, electromagnetic energy fields, and Frisbee flight paths. What do humans understand about us?*

*Are there mailmen in Heaven? If there are, will I have to apologize?*

*I PROMISE DEAR GOD . . . .*

*I will not eat the cats' food before they eat it or after they throw it up.*

*I will not roll on dead seagulls, fish, crabs, etc., just because I like the smell.*

*The sofa is not a face towel.*

*The garbage collector is not stealing our stuff.*

*My head does not belong in the refrigerator.*

*Sticking my nose into someone's crotch is not an acceptable way of saying 'hello'.*

*I do not need to suddenly stand straight up when I'm lying under the coffee table.*

*I must shake the rainwater out of my fur <u>before</u> entering the house.*

*I will not throw up in the car.*

*I will not sit in the middle of the living room and lick my crotch when TV serials are over.*

*The cat is not a squeaky toy; so when I play with him and he makes that noise, its usually not a good thing.*

*And God, when I get to Heaven, can I have my testicles back?*

For as long as I remember, I have loved animals of all kinds. I have had pets when I was young and also immediately after my marriage. So this was a long time gap with no furry creatures around me. Close to 8 yrs. We had been talking about having a dog for some time now, but hadn't got around to it yet, as a direct fall-out of my academic pursuits.

We had put our dreams of having a pet on hold till I completed a grueling fellowship for over a year. There was a constant whine from my younger son about having a dog, with various examples about his friends having a pug, or a Great Dane, or even just a kitten! The stories were endless, and I could see the yearning in his eyes as he talked about it.

Just a month after my course got over, I was browsing through my mail, and I came across this one mail which said there were pups for sale, in Bangalore, and I should contact so and so number. I didn't know if I was ready to look after a third 'dog' after my two sons! So I baulked at the thought of talking to the pet owners or meeting them face to face, and didn't dare call the numbers listed. I preferred doing things online where personal contact was avoided.

So I replied "puppy wanted, preferably, boxer or bulldog or Dalmatian, definitely a female". I didn't expect a reply since I thought such ads are never seen by genuine owners. But to my surprise, three-four people replied! I was now up against the wall and forced to take a decision!

There was a strange thrill coursing through me as I sat down to reply.

There was this one gentleman close to our area, who had boxer pups for sale and we started a communication by e-mail. The mother and father of the pups, were KCI registered (Kennel Club of India), but of course, I only wanted a cute pup for a pet, not some show stopper! He asked me to finally come down and check it out for myself, and we decided to meet up on a Sunday.

# (2)

## *Minx without the meow!*

My baby was introduced to us one bright sunny June Sunday morning, in 2009. She and her sister somersaulted into us the moment the door to their nursery was opened by her human owners! She and her sister were the last of the litter to go. Her brother was already ear-marked to another owner the following day. We had to choose between her and her sister.

Yours truly was the tanner of the two, and the more active one! She sidled up to us as we were reclining on the settee, totally smitten by so many people around . . . . and promptly peed on my leg! We later realized that excitement does that to her and she always looked most apologetic!

Her sister was the hot favorite with the rest of my family, my two sons and my dad. But because 'miss pee-always-on-excitement' was the shorter end of the stick, I insisted on having her as our own . . . . and as usual I got my way! Anyway, I feel she actually chose us and marked us as 'hers'!

I have always loved boxers and I was determined that when I have my own pet again, I would take a boxer, and my sons were, for once, on my side. I had had dogs as pets before, and one thing I knew is that furry dogs were high maintenance! So I was sure I would go in for only a minimum-fur dog, and the boxer, apart from the fact that they had less fur, were also high on the cuteness scale, so it suited me fine. I had looked after a male boxer a few years before, for a family friend who had to go abroad for a month. That dog was such a sweetheart, that I lost my heart forever to all Boxers! Sadly he is no more, after enjoying a blissful 14 yrs. with that loving family.

Now, I admit, that we had not done any extensive research before going in for a dog. We just went by gut instinct. Moreover, I was heady with knowledge that I had had dogs earlier, and couldn't go wrong. I just hadn't bargained for keeping a dog in an apartment! That was a whole new ballgame, but then we managed by making our own rules as we went along!

Wikipedia says, Boxers were bred from the English bulldog and the now extinct Bullenbeiser, but are now said to be a mix of some 18 breeds! They are fawn colored or brindle, with or without white markings, which when extensive, are conventionally called "white" boxers. It is a short-haired breed, with a shiny, smooth coat that lies tight to the body. The recognized colors are accompanied by a white underbelly and white on the front on all four feet. These white markings, are called *flash,* and they often extend onto the neck or face. Brindle refers to a dog with black stripes on a fawn background. A reverse brindle is mistaken as "black" boxer, but there are no pure bred black boxers.

It is renowned from olden times for its great love and faithfulness to its master and the household. It is harmless in the family, but distrustful of strangers, bright and friendly of temperament at play, but brave and determined when aroused. It is the soul of honesty and loyalty, and is very intelligent, modest and clean. They are usually well natured and good-tempered.

They have a naturally abounding energy as a result of this heady concoction of breeds, playful and very good with children. They are active and incredibly strong dogs and require adequate exercise to prevent boredom-associated behaviors such as chewing, digging or licking . . . . which we found out eventually, to our great distress! They have earned a slight reputation of being "headstrong" which can be related to inappropriate obedience training. Owing to their intelligence and working breed characteristics, they typically respond better to positive reinforcement techniques for training.

The boxer is by nature, not an aggressive or vicious breed but, when provoked, is a formidable guardian of any family or home, and like all dogs, requites socialization. They are patient with smaller dogs and puppies, but difficulties with larger adult dogs, especially those of the same sex, may occur. More severe fighting can also occur among female boxers. On average, male boxers are more laid back, while female boxers are a lot more hyperactive.

The term 'boxer' is supposedly derived from the breed's tendency to play by standing on its hind legs, and "boxing" with its front paws, although any such action would likely result in a badly bitten if not broken leg. On the other hand, a German breeder of 40 years' experience states positively that the Boxer does not use its feet, except to try and extinguish a small flame such as a burning match. But a Boxer does box with its head: it will hit (not bite) a cat with its muzzle hard enough to knock it out and will box a ball with its nose. Or perhaps, since the German dictionary translates 'boxer' as 'prize-fighter' the name was bestowed in appreciation of the fighting qualities of the breed rather than its technique.

German linguistic and historical evidence find the earliest written source for the word Boxder in the 18th century, where it is found in a text in the *Deutsches Fremdwörterbuch (The German Dictionary of Foreign Words)*, which cites an author named Musäus of 1782 writing "daß er aus Furcht vor dem großen Baxer salmonet . . . . sich auf einige Tage . . . . At that time the spelling "baxer" equalled "boxer".

In the same vein runs a theory based on the fact that there were a group of dogs known as *Bierboxer* in Munich by the time of the breed's development. These dogs were the result from mixes of Bullenbeisser and other similar breeds. *Bier* (beer) probably refers to the *Biergarten*, the typical Munich beergarden, an open-air restaurant where people used to take their dogs along.

Boxers, like all other dogs, have quite a few health issues, not the least of which is *Boxer Colitis*. It is called this because it most often occurs in Boxers. Boxers who get this are picky eaters and get upset stomachs easily. When they have this problem, their backs are hunched up. The best way to solve this problem is keep the dog on bland food with healthy digestive enzymes. Pancreatic Endocrine Insufficiency is also a common health problem. Basically, this is the Boxer's inability to produce sufficient digestive enzymes and leaves them with upset stomach, even though they are hungry. They have chronic diarrhea and weight loss, but a healthy appetite.

These strong and intelligent animals have been used as service dogs, guide dogs for the blind, therapy dogs, police dogs in K9 units, and occasionally for herding sheep or cattle. The versatility of Boxers was recognized early on by the military, which has used them as valuable messenger dogs, pack carriers, and attack and guard dogs in times of war.

# (3)

## *Love game!*

I picked the pup up and looked into her eyes. They were full of abject devotion for anything human! She promptly licked my nose and wriggled to continue the job up my face! "Here you go," I laughingly passed her onto my younger son, akhilesh, and the pup tried her level best to lick the epidermis off his face!

"It definitely looks like *she* wants to come with us" my elder son, abhishek, commented, on seeing that her sister had now gone off away from us, to explore the area for any tidbits.

And so it came to be. I gave the money to the owners, as my sons were trying their level best to manage a very restless squirming pup from jumping off their arms, where she was being securely ensconced!

Our chosen one had an adorable face, brown all over but for a white patch running from the middle of her chest, right across the left side of her jaw, over to the left side of her nose, and continuing along the middle of her face and ending as a streak of white on her forehead. It definitely gave her a royal look! She could give the most amazing expressions with her eyes and boy, she sure used them to the fullest advantage!

Her journey from the place of her birth to our house in the car was not very eventful, although my sons did their best to give her a rousing time. She was inquisitive but did not like being in an unfamiliar place with a sea of new faces! We took her to the vet en route and all her vaccinations were brought up to date. I also got a whole lot of dog food for her for the ensuing days. She kept wanting to look out of the window and we had kept the shutters down because the AC was on for this hot sunny Sunday morning. After a few tries, she gave up and curled up beside my sons, panting in anxiety.

The car garage led to a small garden. She ran into the grass and promptly relieved herself! Then she sniffed around and gave us a quizzical look as if to ask what's the next move. My younger son dashed across the garden path and she raced after him right into the elevator! Once inside, she looked bewildered!

She lapped up all the milk in her bowl, fast enough on reaching home, and that was about the last day that she ever enjoyed milk! Her disdainful look at the bowlful of milk, subsequently, was a common expression on her face! At one point of time, she did deign to 'like' cold milk but that phase too soon passed! She turned out to be a very fussy eater. All meat based foods were her favorite but the vegetarian kinds, she would royally turn her head away!

Her reluctance to eat any type of vegetarian food except for biscuits, were astounding! She would go hungry for days—yes, we did try that tactic—surviving on love and fresh air only, but refuse to have anything to do with vegetarian food. She did condescend to take toasted bread.

"Let's call her 'bunny'" suggested my dad helpfully.

"No . . . . !" groaned my elder son. "That sounds like we have a rabbit!"

My father grinned apologetically, acknowledging the truth in that.

"How about 'Venus'?" I opined, hesitatingly, coz I knew how vociferously I can be shut down by my sons!

"mmmmmmmmmmmm . . . ." my sons mulled over it.

For a while, we tried that around our new baby. It was 'Venus this' and 'Venus that', until three days later, we all came to the consensus that somehow, 'Venus' just wasn't doing anything for her, and she didn't seem to respond quite well to it.

No name seemed to suit her, or so we thought, because quite a few names were tried on her and discarded. Finally we tried LIZZY! That sort of fitted her and she did respond to it pretty well, since it sat so easy on our tongues and was sharp and sweet! So in effect, she slid into her name and caught onto it very quickly!

Four legs and a barely there tail . . . . that was Lizzy and she made me complete and deliriously happy!

My husband found her adorable when he first laid eyes on her! The fact that Lizzy was so loving and affectionate helped, of course! But he quickly had second thoughts when Lizzy started licking his face!

Her first afternoon was a tad uncomfortable for her in such unfamiliar surroundings, without the proximity of her sibling. However, we tried to get her close to us by, much to the disapproval of my father, having her on our bed! This was to prove our undoing, for Lizzy would always presume this king-sized bed was hers whenever she felt the need to be loved! But Lizzy never whined or moped at being separated from her doggy family.

I had a small 3' by 3' mattress made earlier for my previous pet, and which was thence being used as a futon bed, which I now decided to use for her majesty! She pawed the bed mercilessly for 2 minutes, before settling down. I had just started to drift into my afternoon siesta, it being a holiday on that day, when I heard a low whine. Waiting with baited breath to see if it would progress or settle down, I lay down absolutely still.

Deciding the decibels were not enough to awaken the dead, Lizzy sat up and perched on her haunches and let out a loud wail! I turned over and let my arm down to comfort her and provide the human touch to a lonely soul. She flopped down but continued to emit low decibel plaintive moans! Resigned to my fate, I lifted her up and deposited her on my tummy! She immediately proceeded to lick my face thoroughly, and I had a tough time fighting her affections off!

After a complete lick over, she leapt over onto my side, pawed through a few unforgiving bed sheet bends and let out a huge sigh as she curled up to snooze! I found her puppy face so adorable that I gave in and with my arm over her, I too tried to catch a few winks. Lizzy, her majesty, did not like arms or hands or any such objects over her precious body! She moved away, made her bed again by pawing around and with another huge sigh, flopped happily on it and slept cozily, while I was left looking at her yearningly, because she looked so cute with her puppy face and all. But Lizzy slept blissfully, now that she was close to a human, and warm, with absolutely no idea that I longed to hold her in my arms, completely ensconced against my heart, and shower kisses on her lovely puppy face! Had she any inkling of my violent desires, she probably would have escaped to my sons' room!

"Ma, can we come in?" my sons asked tentatively, standing at the edge of my room door, knowing how vitriolic I get on being woken up mid-sleep! That was Lizzy's cue, she wagged her behind nineteen to the dozen, jumped down from the bed . . . . and without delay relieved herself on the floor! Feeling very reassured, she jumped at my boys and tried to get to their faces to lick!

To be fair to lizzy, there was an almost 2-hour break between her previous episode and this one, for answering nature's call, which was a long break in puppy time! And for all she was concerned, the house was one big bathroom, unless instructed otherwise!

But this brought us to face-to-face with two things— one, Lizzy needs bladder evacuation every time she wakes up or gets excited! Two, she was definitely missing her tail!

We had been advised by the puppy's owners to use newspapers over any soiling, which would absorb the offending material and then clean all the areas in one go with a mop. So that being done, akhilesh sat on the floor to accept Lizzy's enthusiastic greeting, and give some of his own to her!

Lizzy soon forgot her sibling, her parents, her previous owners, everyone, as she settled in with us comfortably, blending into our lifestyle. Her puppy barks and scampering on 4 short legs gave us immense delight and she was the most adored member of the family. The early teething problems of bathroom training were sorted out soon and except for her stubborn eating habits, she was the pampered baby who could no wrong in our eyes!

Lizzy soon realized she could have her way in everything, if she stuck to her guns long enough! She was a happy bundle of hyper-energy, always on the go, with a never-say-die attitude! She was never left alone when we were home. But she was with the maid most of the morning, when we were out at work. She was never tied, so she never learnt to be aggressive at anything or anybody. She had complete faith and implicit trust in humans. She had such a pleasant disposition and such a cute face to go along with it, that it was rather difficult to deny her anything!

Each time we took her to the vet, she sniffed around inquisitively, unlike the other pups and dogs there, who were all apprehensive and reluctant to go in. Each time she received her pricks, we held her close to us, cuddled her so that she did not fear anything and cooed soft nothings into her ear. Lizzy must have thought, humans are weird creatures, making funny noises in a hospital! She did not wince or jerk away when the vet examined her or gave her needle pricks. She bore it stoically and even wagged her tail at the end of it all just to say it was all right, she forgave us! Most times, the vet got a good lick on his face, for being so attentive! At the end of it all, each and every time, we bought Lizzy a squeaky toy from the vet's large collection of toys on display, for being such a sweetheart about it all!

Her heart was so open to new people, new experiences, new creatures. Even at the vet's clinic, she never once pulled her leash to go back, even as a pup. She pulled us in, to smell and meet all the new dogs and other animals there! Very accommodating!

The one thing she never tired of was playtime! Every waking moment for her, nay every second in her life, was to play, and to play like she had a trophy to win! There were no half measures with Lizzy! She played to win! Even as a pup, her strength was extraordinary. Abhishek, my elder son, has lost many a game of tug-of-war with her, when he was a hulking 60 kg and she was a mere 20 kg! It was just attitude! Lizzy had to be tops! Her play was always accompanied by growls and frowns and snaps! But she never bit anyone in anger, and if ever her teeth nipped us accidentally, she was profuse in her apologies, licking us and curling up in our laps in abject surrender, so embarrassed to have let her teeth do the talking! Many times, just to tease her, I have whined plaintively, to make her think she bit me! Lizzy immediately stops whatever she was doing, drops any toy she was holding, and runs across to lick and console me!

Her choicest reactions were reserved for Sunday mornings, when I got meat for her! Since we were strict vegetarians, and Lizzy got vegetarian meals all through the week, I got either mutton or chicken or fish for her on Sundays, the days I was off from work. Lizzy must have thought I was the greatest hunter there ever was! I went out empty handed and returned half hour later, with the juiciest pieces of meat for her with no effort! But Lizzy had to wait for the next 3 hrs. to actually dig into it because it was boiled and then cooled before it was served to her. Lizzy was very impatient in such matters, especially when the smell wafted in through the mosquito meshing of the door, which remained shut till such time as it cooled! She could see it, smell it, but she could not eat it! Boy! That riled and rankled her no end! I kept the door shut because Lizzy picks up the pieces from the pot while it is still hot and gobbles it up . . . . and then brings it all out again, including some food that she ate 2 days back, since she cannot keep lumps of boiling meat in her tummy!

But smelling the succulent meat across the door and not being able to have it, drives her totally bonkers! She will sit close to the door, and bark plaintively, with a catch in her voice, just to tell us that she is morally hurt by our attitude! If that doesn't work, she will whine loudly, fit to wake up the dead! If that doesn't work either, she will paw the door and try to bite it in complete frustration! If by chance, the maid leaves any window of opportunity, like when she goes out to hang the clothes and leaves even an inch of the door open, Lizzy will wiggle through and pounce on the meat! I cannot remember any Sunday without such an incident, thanks to Lizzy's tomfoolery!

# (4)

## *Boxing around!*

Lizzy came to us with a stump of a tail! Her owners had already cut the tail to a short vestige, as is normally done in boxers. My sons always regretted not seeing a nice long tail on Lizzy.

"Dogs are meant to wag their tails! Not humans!" abhishek remarked scathingly. "Why would anyone want to mess with nature! And anyway, the choice should be left to the final owners, not the litter owners!"

"Yeah, but you see one can never be sure at what age the pup is taken by a new owner, by which time it may be too late to snip the tail. And, if its not done at birth, then it starts bleeding and that's a whole new chapter nobody wants to start!" I replied.

"Yeah ok. But why not just leave a lovely tail!" he continued protesting. "it looks so inelegant and ungainly to see a stump!" he snorted derisively.

For her part, Lizzy did not feel the loss of an organ, the source of so much discontent among her human owners. She compensated by shaking her whole 'derrière' when the occasion arose, which was quite often! Like all animals, Lizzy lived with what she got, no regrets.

She was the most loving creature, always forgiving, and loved every variety of humankind, especially kids. She was wary of all the four-legged creatures around, which were bigger than her. But she loved to chase all smaller living beings and cats were her favorite! At the age she was in, nipping and play fighting engrossed her! Chewing all things fascinated her! We soon taught her to spit out all chewables so that she would not end up eating the rubber slippers and cardboard boxes.

"Lizzy dirty! Lizzy cheee . . . ! Lizzy drop it!"

Poor girl, she would get the fright of her life on being assaulted by all these loud screaming admonishes! But she soon got the hang of it and obediently started spitting out all the offensive ingredients. It was the same story on the road. Anything disgusting, which animals are wont to smell eagerly, she would jump back as if a snake had struck her, realizing there would be serious consequences to further investigating the said disgusting object!

Chasing an object around the house as it moved away from her was the most amusing sport for her! Especially so if it made an offending noise! One of her favorites was empty cheese tins. They would roll away from her and make a goddamn awful screeching noise on the floor as she dragged it, or boxed it around with her nose or sometimes her forehead, and that gave her immense pleasure! But it gave us the most terrible headache!

There was this one evening . . . . Lizzy was at it in the evening with her tin toy! She obviously felt the house was too quiet and decided to up the decibel quite a bit! She butted the tin box all over the living room floor, making the same goddamn awful screeching noise, that destroyed any peace of mind left! She contributed to the cacophony by her own insistent barks and growls! Soon, the tin disappeared into my son's bedroom, under his bed! Lizzy bent down and barked at it for good measure, admonishing it for disappearing from her eagle eyes and grabby paws! She was astounded that the 'toy' did not listen to her threats and come out! Lizzy followed the toy to its hiding place, trying to squeeze her ample frame under the bed. Lucky for her, and for the decibel levels in the house, the 'toy' was not very deep under and she managed to grab a hold of it with her teeth.

She then chased the 'toy' back into the living room and managed to push it into my bedroom which has wooden floors, this time. The awful screeching noise changed to a dull scrappy sound, which made us all wince in agony! Unfortunately, the darned 'toy' slipped underneath the steel bureau! Oh Lizzy did not like that one bit! She kneeled down looked under. It was quite deep inside and Lizzy did not get a good look-see! She was affronted!

She jumped onto the bed and from her vantage point, she tried to see the offending item. She could not!

She barked at it loudly. It did not come out. She jumped down and angled herself under the bureau and tried to blindly paw the 'toy' back to her loving jaws! By this time, she had herself an adoring audience. My sons settled on the bed and cheered from the sidelines, deciding this was going to go on for a while and it was better to get some entertainment! They kept a safe distance away from irritated Lizzy, who had no respect for 'obstacles' in her path when she was excited and hell-bent on doing 'justice' to her toys!

Lizzy barked and then whined and alternated this for a while, hoping I would help out! She then sat back and looked at me accusingly. "What the hell is wrong with you? Cant you see my 'toy' has escaped my clutches and I desperately want it back! Do something for cryin' out loud woman!"

I accepted defeat. I went over to the bureau bottom. Lizzy moved back, licking her lips expectantly. I bent over and retrieved the 'toy' out. I held it tantalizingly towards Lizzy. She looked at it, then looked at me. We had been over this earlier, many times. She knew I never gave it to her so easily!

I pretended the 'toy' had limbs. I slowly 'walked' it towards her and tapped it on her nose and then quickly hid it under the bureau, before she could grab it! Lizzy started barking and thumping her front legs, trying to jump on it, the way she does when she wants to subdue an actively moving prey! I repeated this maneuver a couple of times. Lizzy kept up a constant barking and jumping, getting all rattled and angry! She was salivating now but enjoying all the play time!

I relented finally, much to the disappointment of my audience and Lizzy grabbed the toy out of my hands, before I had second thoughts! She then triumphantly trotted to the living room, to start the game again!

It would annoy her to see her favorite chew toy slipping underneath the settee. She would paw and growl and bark at it in vain, but nothing would come of it. Finally with a huge sigh, and a mournful expression on her baby face, she would look up at us and whine! She would make sure that our attention was diverted to the task at hand, her hand i.e., and whine plaintively at the settee bottom. That was the cue!

"Ma, I am not getting it out", my elder son warned me, seeing my attempts at getting his attention to help Lizzy out. "If she is dumb enough to slide it inside, that's her problem" he retorted, upon seeing me frown at his refusal.

"She is just a baby! What do you expect! We did worse for you guys when you were babies!" I retaliated.

"Ma, she keeps doing it. She has to know that she has to get it out herself!" he protested. Realizing I was slowly starting to lose my grip on my ever-so-short temper, he groaned and reluctantly with obvious displeasure, bent down to retrieve the object.

That was Lizzy's cue! Just as he was bending down, she lovingly give his face a big wet slurp!

"Jeez!" abhishek shrieked, on being thoroughly licked on the face. Lizzy saw her chance and completed the job on seeing abhishek's exposed face! She climbed onto his back and gave his head also a good measure of her love when abhishek tried to put his face down to avoid her wet licks! After a considerably long and exhausting revelry, the chew toy was finally retrieved and Lizzy sat down happily to resume her job of destroying the toy, while abhishek proceeded to wash his face, with distaste.

This was a regular feature each time somebody tried helping Lizzy to retrieve something from under the settee. In time, my younger son, akhilesh, devised a method of covering his face and offering only his back for Lizzy's attack! The moment he bent down, Lizzy would launch herself, all four paws on the back and try her level best to get access to the face, failing which she would run riot on the scalp hair, which would have disastrous consequences in case that person happened to me or any other lady with well coiffured hair!

It was a common occurrence for Lizzy to somehow manage to put the same chew toy under the same settee in the same sitting repeatedly. And then sit back and bark for all she was worth! Soon I noticed that my sons, who normally sat in the living room to study or to watch TV, started disappearing from the vicinity of Lizzy's play! It started innocently enough.

"Ma I am going to study in my room," abhishek would announce, getting up from the couch, and hurrying into his room.

He must have gestured with his eye to akhilesh, coz soon enough, "Ma I am doing my homework in my room," would be the rejoinder from the younger sibling.

"But its nice to just sit here, all of us, and study," I protested, slowly taking my head out of my mammoth medical book. But I was talking to their backs.

"Woof, woof!" Lizzy announced. "Oh, keep it quiet Lizzy," I growled back.

Lizzy, not one to keep quiet when her favorite chew toy was underneath akhilesh's couch, set up a loud whine! I jumped out of my skin in fright! "Lizzy! Would you mind? Hard working people are trying to study here!" I admonished.

Undeterred, her whines reached a feverish pitch, as she kept giving me pitiful looks. Now Lizzy, we all knew, was a big drama queen who would have made Elizabeth Taylor blush! But boy, she looked so cute, and I was such a sucker for boxer faces!

I looked around for my two helpers, but apparently they had prior knowledge about Lizzy's predicament, and had so obviously slipped out of the room, and now I realized why! In resignation, I heaved my hefty medical book aside, and slid under the couch to retrieve the toy . . . . only to have yours truly launch herself on me!

To say that I was unprepared, was putting it mildly! It was like a washing machine doing its job on you! She licked every piece of open skin available, and then some!

"Lizzy stop!" I screamed. "You get off me right this minu . . . te . . . ." I couldn't even complete my sentence because Lizzy was trying her best to get access to my mouth and I was desperately trying to keep her face from getting into my mouth! I covered my face with my hands, which were so far outstretched underneath the couch. So she decided to re-arrange my hair! I was furious, I latched onto her squirming body with my left hand and held her tightly. With my right hand I managed to get the toy out and retreated to the safety of my couch, on top of it, Lizzy still clutched tightly in the crook of my arm!

"Woof!" she yelped into my ear.

"Ah . . . . Lizzy is happy now that she has her toy."

I looked up to see abhishek grinning lopsidedly from the entrance to his room.

"Ma, don't get angry. Its just a 'poor baby', murmured akhilesh, sarcasm dripping from every word, ducking to avoid the chew toy thrown at him by me!

I glared at them furiously. "You guys jolly well sit here from hence forth and its your responsibilities to get the toy out if its under your respective chairs!" I admonished.

"Ah, go take a walk, Ma!" retorted my sons in unison, disappearing into their rooms.

"Lizzy, behave. You get your toy in, you get it out. No amount of drama is gonna make me do it again. Got that!" I said sternly to Lizzy. Lizzy decided there was too much excitement going around! So she curled up by my side on the couch.

After about 5 minutes, I hear a low whine. And there was Lizzy again, on the ground, looking around the center table . . . . you guessed it, for her lost toy!

# (5)

*Cat games!*

**H**er appetite remained the same, but she was growing by leaps and bounds. She became tall and gangly, all legs and no body! Neighbors would exclaim in amazement at how big she became by the time they saw her after 2-3 days gap.

She was an absolutely spoilt brat, as my family would say, and they insisted it was because I exercised discipline only for humans and not for dogs, and definitely not for

Lizzy! Lizzy would never bite us, but she growled and barked and made warning noises for all she was worth! One thing she was afraid of was my stern voice, which would make her cringe into a corner, curled up like a ball . . . . and there would immediately be a bathroom mishap, in her anxiety! There was never a day when she would put up resistance to a scolding or threaten us back. And the only reason she would get scolded was, for her fussy eating!

Gradually we started taking her for longer walks. Initially, she would crowd around my legs when I took her out of the neighborhood she was familiar with, and any vigorous barking would send her into a fright. But she soon came out of that, and started walking nonchalantly, sniffing curiously at all the muck Indian roads abound in. But woe betide any sightings of a cat! Unless her leash was very tightly secured around my hand, she would shoot off in a flash, dragging anybody latched onto her. Many a time, I have 'flown' with her, literally!

There were a lot of tomcats in our neighborhood and to Lizzy's delight they would choose that very moment when she was out for a walk, to cross the road! Lizzy's eyes bulged in angst—the audacity of it all, as Lizzy would say, walking and running in front of a Dog!

There was this one time, when I was in a hurry to get back home, to go to work, and possibly a little distracted because of that. A rather small cat happened to cross the road, and before I could say 'hallelujah' Lizzy was off!

"Lizzy! Sto . . . . oooop!" I yelped but she had wriggled out of her body collar and was racing across the road, jumping over the fence, looping across the hedge, taking a flying leap into somebody's ground floor balcony, where the poor cat was cringing and mewing! I was left with a leash and no dog at the end of it!

I ran in the same direction, thinking the worst, and wondering what kind of mayhem she must have created! Of course, I didn't dare jump all those obstacles, which Lizzy sailed over so effortlessly!

"Lizzy!" I yelled, when I caught a blur of brown fur. "Don't you dare!" I continued, still running to catch up with her. I came to an abrupt halt as I encountered an unusual sight. There was Lizzy sitting on her haunches in front of a very angrily hissing cat! Lizzy pawing in the air at the cat now and then playfully, with her front paw, and then jerking back in shock when the cat's claws made contact with her soft paw.

"Lizzy, no. Do not do anything" I commanded.

Lizzy looked up at me.

"Woof! Its playtime momma, chill out" she seemed to say, and took the classical pose to invite the cat to play, rump in the air, and front paws bent low, and face at the level of the cat's face. To say that the cat was anything but prepared to see a huge lopping face with tongue hanging out so close to its nose, was putting it mildly! The cat let out a loud hiss and jumped over the balcony railing in fright!

"Lizzy stop! No jumping!" I hissed sternly, hoping not to wake up the owners of the flat. I slowly slid the collar over Lizzy and held her tight. She looked at me quizzically. "I have a perfect playmate, and you *have* to be the spoilsport!" she curled up her nose in indignance.

Luckily the commotion had not invited any unwanted attention and I thankfully made good my escape. "Bad girl, Lizzy" I reprimanded her sternly, clutching her leash tightly to avoid a second mishap that morning.

Lizzy looked rather apologetic and kept throwing furtive glances at my face, hoping for a smile here and there. I kept my face turned away from her, totally affronted, that she should just take off like that leaving me embarrassed! Lizzy kept a low profile, slinking around my legs, trying to fathom if my mood had improved, and also worried about the consequences once she reached home and was within my hand's reach.

But that was just it! Lizzy can scream bloody murder at the cats, but at heart, she was a doll! She could not harm any living thing. Everything and everybody was just a playmate. She could not harm anybody even if she wanted to, coz she just didn't know how! She was a good soul.

As we entered the lift, I noticed how quiet and subdued this mischievous bundle of unending energy had become, and my heart melted. I gave a small smile. Lizzy has this unerring sixth sense that tells her exactly when I am in a better mood! She slowly sniffed the air, not looking at me, as if she was doing something important. And there was just the tiniest bit of a wag on her stump of a tail, as she slowly turned her head and looked at me with those big brown soulful eyes. I gave a half smile, and that was her cue! She jumped up and placed her front paws on my waist, yearning to lick my face, trying to get air-borne! How quickly she had discerned that I had forgiven her, and was ever ready to make amends! In a dog's world, there were no hard feelings. We are here to give and receive love, they seem to say.

If I had thought that Lizzy had learnt her lesson and would start behaving herself on the road, I was sadly mistaken. For Lizzy, the previous day's happenings were to be forgotten by the end of that day, no hard feelings!

Anything that moved on the road was an affront to her being a dog! Any movement on the ground or air, would cause her to stiffen up, sniff the air expectantly, detect a faint smell of a cat / squirrel / field rat / bird / cow / lizard . . . . and just about anything, and that would set her off in a frenzy! She was wont to lift one of her fore legs and stand absolutely still on three legs, while she made up her mind from which direction she would launch her attack!

The first time she detected a squirrel scurrying up a tree, she was shocked! The hair on her back stood up as she realized there were small fleshy, furry, creatures that could travel against gravity! That irritated her no end. From that moment on, each time she passed that tree, she would stop, lift a foreleg, sniff relentlessly, and then launch herself up the tree!

When she first did it, I was so unprepared, that I let go of her leash! Lizzy jumped up the tree, held onto the lowest branch for dear life, and as gravity would have her way, fell down onto the soft grass below, in a very ungainly fashion! She quickly shook herself off the dirt, with nary a squeak, although it must have been a hard fall from a fair height, even if there was grass below. Luckily there were no broken bones and no major skin wounds either.

She then, immediately, looked up to see where the dratted squirrel had escaped to!

Lizzy had such a one-track devotion to the task at hand, when it involved subduing a smaller scurrying animal, that it came close to obsession! I had to pull on her leash with all my might, to get her to move away from the tree! I have often wondered what Lizzy would do if I left her there, whether she would wait at the foot of the tree to get the squirrel in her sights and then launch an aerial attack, or try attempting to get onto the tree when she gets the smell of the squirrel or rat on the tree, and then go for the kill! But would she wait a full day for such an attempt or give up after a couple of hours. Alas, I do not have a garden big enough to have a tree with squirrels to try this experiment!

# (6)

## *Nature calls!*

We had the devil of the time toilet training Lizzy! For one, she had a mighty loose bladder and any and every stimulus could set her off! "Thank God, she is not a male!" I proclaimed with a heart-felt sigh, "or else, we would have dog pee on all the wall edges, 24x7!"

We used to take her down every 2 hrs. and make her go in the grass downstairs. After a few days, we didn't even have to whisper "Lizzy shoo shoo!" She would sniff around and promptly sit down to relieve herself! The 'fun' started if we overshot her 2hrly schedule! We would have to hurry her into the elevator, literally nudging her into it, coz if left on her own for even a few seconds, Lizzy would sit down in front of the elevator doors and relieve herself comfortably, oblivious to our frantic hisses!

Many a time, we have had to face the agony of hurrying her down in a frenzy and then . . . . having to see her squat to pee blissfully right inside the elevator! We would then have to trudge all the way up, clean up the mess with copious rolls of tissue paper and then wipe it clean with a mop, coz I didn't want the neighbors to comment on our having a dog, which dirties the surroundings. Moreover, ethically, and morally, we didn't like to leave dog poo all around, whether in liquid or solid form!

When school started, we were faced with the dilemma whether to 'train' my part-time maid to take Lizzy down, or to allow Lizzy her way and use the house as the general open air bathroom! My maid found it very funny and embarrassing to take Lizzy down for her job and so we decided to train her to do it in one of the bathrooms.

Lizzy picked that up very quickly too and she would run to the bathroom, with a very concentrated look on her face, heading straight, not distracted by any noise or happenings, till she had relieved herself in the bathroom! Of course, we had to run after her and hose the mess down, coz if left too long, the bathroom would start to smell something awful! Besides Lizzy had no compunctions about stepping on the mess as she grandly made her way out of the bathroom with a pleased look on the face, and I certainly didn't want the entire flat to smell like one big urinal! So we had to hose down her paws before she stepped daintily out. But we made sure to praise her to the heavens each time she peed outside the house or in the bathroom, and not inside the flat. It was like a pee-party!

My husband was not too happy about his (our) bathroom being used by the house dog! Especially since he had a very sensitive nose and did not take kindly to the 'stink' as he put it! I started using the room freshener rather copiously, after Lizzy's sojourns into the bathroom. But somehow, my husband's nostrils would flare in disgust as soon as he sniffed the air inside and realized that Lizzy had just spent the last 30 seconds there!

What ever the training, lizzy *refused* to use the bathroom when we were not at home!

So actually the whole purpose was defeated! We found pools of pee in strategic places in the house, the third room, being the favorite! She especially 'liked' the carpet and the door mat! So the carpet was dry-cleaned and rolled up, never to be used till such time as Lizzy was 'shoo shoo' trained! Which turned out to be 'never' because she insisted on using the carpet if we ever sneaked it out for a guest or any other occasion! She especially targeted the bathroom door mat. But would never go into the bathroom to actually do the job!

We tried everything, scolding her after dragging her to the 'accidents', beating the stick on the floor next to her, making an awful racket so that she would know that she could be at the end of that stick if she repeated her 'accidents! But it didn't really work. She would just skulk away on seeing us even before we became aware of the misdemeanors! It was actually comical to see her delight on having us come back home, and then suddenly realize what a whole lot of mess she had made in the house, and so gingerly creep away from the reach of our hands. Her favorite place was between the couches! And the moment she heard one of us scream that we'd inadvertently stepped onto one of her pee areas or big jobs, she would start trembling.

She never retaliated when we banged the stick on the floor for all we were worth! Her pleading eyes and the looks she gave us from the corners of her eyes, were all the reaction she gave on encountering 3 mad people shouting and screaming and flaying a wooden stick onto the ground, like some ancient tribal ritualistic dance! What she must be thinking in her doggy brain! What a fuss these 2-legged creatures make just for attending nature's call, ranting and shaking their heads in fury and waving a funny stick around!

The boys hated coming back from school without me around, coz they knew that a whole lot of cleaning awaited them! In fact, they took turns each day for the cleaning up, and it sometimes would remain like that for hours till such time that the person whose duty it was to clean that day, returned from school or whatever other job he had! So if I happened to reach home before the person 'on duty' did, I would walk bang into fumes that hit me the moment I entered the house, and predictably, that would get me all riled up!

Luckily, for all our peace of minds, Lizzy didn't budge from her bed at night, and slept soundly, some on her bed and some on mine, without professing the need for bathroom breaks during the night. Even on Sundays, when we all slept in late, Lizzy would be stretched out cozily on the bed. But of course, the moment we got up, we had to rush her into the bathroom, or else face a puddle on the floor next to the bed! She has rarely, if ever, peed on the bed.

Her trysts with the bathroom were legendary. If we had a guest coming in, there would be frantic shouts to Lizzy first!

"Lizzy come fast, the bathroom," we would insist. Lizzy would be torn between wanting to plant herself bodily on the guest desperately, and heeding to our anxious calls. It was comical the way she would stand undecided next to the door, her face turned towards us but her attention on the front door.

"Lizzy! You come right now or they will be hell to pay!" I would yell. That Lizzy knew was true in every sense of the word! So she would scurry in, pee a little, look up at me, wag her tail stump, and not finding a companionable demeanor on my exterior, she would turn around, pee some more and then race out of the bathroom door to greet the newcomer. Of course, it goes without saying that even after her sojourn in the bathroom, she would still manage to pass a few drops in her excitement, on my spotless living room floor, on greeting the human! That obviously would incur my wrath and Lizzy would scrounge up behind the newcomer hoping for a reprieve! This would go on unfailingly each time we had someone over, even my maid who came at 8 am each day! Lizzy's greeting would be boisterous and have an equal reaction from her rear end! Of course, her big jobs were almost never done inside the premises of the house, thankfully.

Puppy chow meant three meals a day. But since I was almost never home till evening, we trained Lizzy, once she became over 6 months, to sustain on two large meals a day. Mostly I fed her!

Lizzy did not like food! Boy, that was the understatement of the century!!

Not the vegetarian kind, at least.

Anything sweet, or salty, or meat-like, she wolfed down in a jiffy, but everything else, was met with utter scorn! I literally fed her, as in pried her mouth open and stuffed a handful of food inside, without which, Lizzy would have been skin and bones only! I wonder if that construed as animal abuse!

Initially there was stiff resistance from her. More was spat out than retained in. But I soon overcame that, and Lizzy settled down to suffer this feat also. Not to say that she liked it. Of boy, she didn't!

She would try and hide each time food was placed in her bowl and she knew I was coming to drag her to her bowl. It became a drama each day, each meal. I would put her meal in the bowl, and Lizzy would scurry into the farthest corner of the entire flat! But I soon learned that if I didn't pay any attention to her or her food, she came back to investigate what the hell was wrong with her family today which left her to go hungry! The moment I met her eye, she would curl into a ball, wait for the moment and soon decide that, my elder son, abhishek was the best offer of protection from my predator hands!

Abhishek yelped in agony the first time lizzy leapt onto his lap!

"Lizzy! Would you mind? That's my book you are destroying! Lizzy!

There he was sitting cozily on his single couch, his legs askew and lolling off the couch, trying to study and catch some shut eye at the same, (which he disclaims), and then, out of nowhere, this ball of fur, lands bang onto his middle! It was like a penalty shoot-out with the football! And Lizzy didn't mind where her paws and face landed, as long as she kept her body curled up and away from my 'tentacles'!

"Aw, Lizzy! Watch it! Take your dirty paws out!" was his constant moan.

Apparently once bitten twice shy, because after that episode, every meal time, abhishek would scrounge up into a small ball hoping to be unnoticeable to Lizzy! But that hardly stopped her! She would still leap onto whatever was the exposed portion available to her!

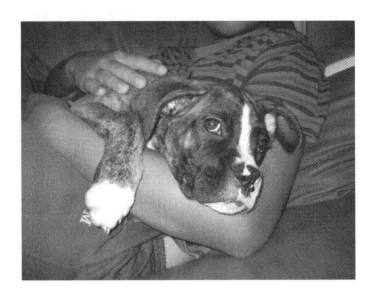

I let her believe that there was protection from abhishek, and so I wouldn't drag her for a while. A little later, she would forget and slink down off abhishek, to occupy another recess in the hall, and then I would make my move!

"Lizzy, my darling baby," I crooned softly, so as to not scare her. Lizzy looked at me very suspiciously, knowing fully well that I was not given to such drooling affection when she had refused food kept in her bowl. I had to grab her firmly then, under her arms and carry her on her two hind legs to her bowl, all the while kissing her and cuddling her, coz she was such a sweetheart and she had such a sweet doggy smell! There I had to hold her while I coaxed, cajoled, forced her to have her meal.

There were various enticements that I had in my armament. I had to vary these enticements, depending on my time constraint and her hunger levels! The one that she loved most was of course the beef / chicken jerky pieces. She tolerated the cheese bits, but she took an awful long time to decide it was palatable, after much prolonged sniffing and appraisals!

"Ma, your kissing her is also torture for her!" my sons would remark slyly. "The dance of death", abhishek said dramatically!

"I know! First you kiss her . . . ."started akhilesh.

"The kiss of death!" announced abhishek dramatically.

". . . . and then you smother her in your arms till she can hardly breathe!" continued akhilesh. "And then you kiss her some more. And to top it all, you crush her and then torture her with unwanted food! Mamma, you could teach the Chinese some new methods of torture!"

Nothing deterred my determination to feed Lizzy. I admit I was overzealous, because Lizzy was none the worse for it! Whatever fatty food I stuffed down her gullet, she refused to put on more weight and it remained an even 25kg, come what may! She was generally so active and so agile, that she burned up all her calories and always appeared lean and fit! I had even got a whole skew of blood tests done for her, in case she was 'hyperthyroid' or maybe diabetic. But she came out with flying colors in all her tests!

Obviously whatever went in, had to find a way out, and Lizzy firmly believed that every walk meant that she had to pass off a little of whatever went into her! So even if she was taken out every 2-3 hrs. Lizzy would still do her big job! It was only later we came to know, thanks to the internet, that it was because her digestion was not good, and that was due to lack of adequate pancreatic enzymes. She came down to 2 big jobs a day after supplementary pancreatic enzymes were started.

Apparently Lizzy did not believe in the adage, "age makes one wiser and better", because even as she grew older, mealtimes were a repetition of her puppy stage and there was never a time that I actually saw her eat her meal, which was not meat-based, on her own.

"Leave her for 1-2 days and she will come around to eating on her own. How you fuss!" was what my husband always, unfailingly, threw at me, each time he saw the laborious drama for her morning meals. His scorn was brushed aside with utmost nonchalance, because it never did make a dent in my morning routines with Lizzy! With time, even he stopped commenting and would merely give a wry smile and look heavenwards for divine retribution! God they say, has a special place for animals in His kingdom and Lizzy was definitely one of the chosen ones, because, she would fast for days without any ill effects unless it was lumped into her mouth!

# (7)

## *Vigor & spice!*

"Lizzy . . . . y . . . y . . . stop racing up the stairs! You'll hit somebody coming down! Come back here!" The only response to all my entreaties was a blur of brown as Lizzy raced up the stairs, instead of taking the lift up to our third floor apartment, while I slowly made my way up by the stairs.

"Lizzy you are so grounded for life!" I would snap at her as soon as I reached the 3rd floor landing, hoping to find a remorseful pup, but her majesty would be waiting for me impatiently in the third floor foyer.

"Woof woof!" was all she had time to say to me as she bounded up the final set of stairs, two at a time, to reach the terrace, always squeezing in a second to fling a glance back at me, to make sure I was following up!

"Hurry up! I don't have all day, you know!" her looks indicated!

This was her all time favorite place since it was open and spacious, unlike the claustrophobic confines of the flat below.

Lizzy would go positively mad on reaching the terrace! They were divided into four sections, one above each flat in the third floor. I was always careful to restrict her to my side of the terrace because I had faced the testiness of the neighbors in all other things! But how can one limit the exuberance of a four month old, four legged bundle of extreme energy! She had to, just had to, circle the terrace at F1 speeds, always rounding the bends and never even once hitting a corner! Very occasionally, she would trespass into the adjoining terrace. On that occasion, the owners to whom the terrace 'belonged', had instructed the security guard to warn me against such future infringements on their territory, because Lizzy, apparently gave their terrace a lot of 'wear and tear' and their terrace flooring was giving away! What can you say? I strictly kept Lizzy away from 'encroaching'!

She would go ballistic on seeing crows perched on the terrace wall and charge at them, skidding to a halt as they teasingly flew away, in a low arch, and then returned to the same point. She never once hit the wall, even if she approached the crows at lightening speeds!

"Woof woof woof" was all the deep-throated accompaniment there was, to her charge at them, but the crows were past master at this game and would harass her endlessly.

Fortunately, Lizzy did not have the irritating habit of barking ceaselessly, as some dogs do, especially the smaller ones. So that was a big relief, not only to me but also to the neighbors, I have no doubt! At the most, she would bark once or twice to convey the ulterior message and then leave the adversary to take note of her size and keep the hell out of the territory! Besides, she had a nice baritone bark, which did not irritate the ears, but definitely resonated!

As Lizzy was pre-occupied with the crows, I would utilize this chance to grab the object she had brought up with her in her jaws, a stick or a coconut or her favorite, a plastic bottle!

"Lizzy! 1 . . . . 2 . . . . 2 . . . ." I would stop tantalizingly, and then "3 . . . . !!" With that I would throw the 'ball' as far as possible for her to fetch back. Sometimes for good measure, I would also race behind it, and Lizzy would charge at the ball, forgetting the crow for the moment, grab the 'ball' and hold it in her jaws with a triumphant expression in her face, panting to take deep breaths. This was the everyday exercise that both of us had begun to love and appreciate, since the rest of the day would be spent inside four walls with hardly any moving around.

We would keep at this for just 10 minutes but if the sun was not overhead and there was a cool breeze wafting across, I would leave Lizzy there on the terrace and proceed to do my day's work in the kitchen, since I had two school going children to cater to. Lizzy would run around, chasing crows and imaginary squirrels, till she could not stand the brutal rays of the rising sun. She had to, then slowly trudge down, wearily, panting for all she was worth. The door to the house was left open for her majesty to make her way in, when she felt the need!

She would enter the house, glance over at me to ensure I had not deserted her totally, lap up an entire bowl of water always kept fresh for her, and then flop heavily onto the floor in front of the kitchen sighing contently. Totally spent and happy in her world, she would soon drift in and out of sleep, always keeping one eye on me and follow me with her eyes, in case I left the premises of the kitchen!

Morning times were always rushed, since all three of us had to leave at around the same time. So I had to invariably, gallop in and out of rooms to get all the jobs done. Lizzy did not like it one bit! It meant she had to leave her cozy corner each time and follow me around, lest I leave her and go, like I do each day when I leave to go to my work. She did not like me out of her eye range.

So it was a constant sight for my sons to see me rushing in and out of the kitchen with Lizzy in hot pursuit! "Sit down sweetie. You don't have to follow me, I am not leaving yet." I would croon, and look up to see my sons glowering at me!

"She doesn't really understand you, you know! She is just being a dog!"

"She does understand and probably more than you two brats ever did!" I would snap back. "At least she understands the tone and puts two and two together, which is more than I can say for you two!"

"Yeah right. Yes mama, she really understands everything! God, some 'elders' are so naïve!" he would lament.

"Oh yeah, she is gonna say 'mama' soon, just you wait!"

With both my sons choking on their breakfast after that remark, I would escape into the kitchen, with Lizzy hot on my tail.

"You will too, won't you my darling," and Lizzy would look up adoringly at me, licking her lips gently, in acknowledgement of the love and attention. Lizzy basked in all the love I showered and had become my shadow completely.

She always slept on her bed by the side of my cot. My sons have, many a time, enticed her at night, to sleep with them, even on their single beds, foregoing their individual comforts for the cuddly feeling Lizzy gave. Lizzy would go along with their cajoling, stay with them for a few minutes, and then slink into my room and flop onto her bed, after a cursory sniff at me, to ensure I was there. No amount of further entreaties, would make her go to their room. Finally, if she felt threatened by the tone of their voices constantly beckoning her, she would jump on to my bed and cuddle up close to me, keeping one eye open for any intrusions by the boys! After a while, re-assured by my sleeping presence, she would jump off and occupy some corner of the room, on the floor, sometimes, if it was a hot night, or on her mattress, if she wanted something soft.

I would sometimes hear her moving during the night, shaking herself on and off, and then trudging off to the living room, to curl up on the settee. This was often her favorite place, whether in the morning or in the night, since the all-encompassing structure of the settee gave her a secure feeling and the material was soft enough to give her a comfortable shut-eye. Since the settees were designated per person, my sons, at all other times, would nudge her slowly down to occupy it themselves. Too much fuss in throwing her out, would invite my wrath, so they had to do it slyly! Lizzy was accommodative if nothing else and would promptly go on to the next empty settee, to be dislodged again impatiently! She would finally settle on my large settee, where she would lie undisturbed. But the largeness of the settee did not give her the security that a single chair gave. So Lizzy never missed a chance to jump onto an unoccupied single settee any time!

Her vantage position was on top of the backrest of any one of the settees, where she would perch and preen! Since the top of the backrest was rather broad, it was easy for her to plant her body there in comfort and observe all the happenings in the vicinity, getting a bird's eye view of everything. She would even take a short nap there, but rouse up immediately if there was some noise in the background, and crane her neck to elicit information about any threat to her family!

Customarily, every day, by early morning, she trudged back to the warmth of my bed and curled up contently at my foot. And this is how I find her each day when I wake up to the urgent calls of my mobile alarm.

The sound of the alarm, would rouse up Lizzy too, and she would stretch herself languidly on my bed, and then slide across to my sleepy face, to give it a thorough face-wash, before I could say 'Hallelujah'! I then cradle her in my arms, across my abdomen, and proceed to give her a complete 'kiss-wash' as my sons have labeled it! I cant stop crushing her and kissing her, because, as dogs go, Lizzy had a sweet honey-suckle smell to her, and we all couldn't get enough of it! With that much love, our mornings start!

Lizzy had an all-enthusiastic exuberant approach to everything in life except food . . . . of the vegetarian kind ie! She had an equally excited reaction to going down the stairs to go out, as coming up them! Every morning, between 6 and 6.30 am we would go out for the walk. I firmly believed in exercising my pet, which I took it as good exercise for the owner too. It is said that if the pet in the house is obese, the owner is not getting enough exercise! So we would manage about half hour worth of walking and then I would roll the ball around for Lizzy's exercise. This kept her fit as a fiddle.

We always took the elevator, after a bad experience one time.

Initially, in the early puppy days, Lizzy was a little apprehensive of the elevator, especially when the steel doors closed. So I took to going down by stairs, and being the hyperactive dog that she was, Lizzy tore down the stairs, and I let go of the leash for fear of tripping myself!

One day . . . . there was a blood curdling yell in ten seconds of her travelling down, which set me racing down, two steps at a time! I was greeted by this petrified lady in the first floor lobby, and a very quizzical Lizzy, who kept turning her face left and right wondering why this human was making hypersonic noises when all she wanted was to play with her!

"Lizzy stop right there!" I hissed at her.

"Sorry" this was to the stupefied lady. "She is just a pup and won't do anything."

The words were not even out of my mouth when I see an excited Lizzy trying to effusively greet this new human, whom she obviously took as my friend, since I was supposedly having a tete-e-tete with her.

"Yeah, but does the 'pup' know that!" the lady whispered.

"Sorry sorry, so terribly sorry" this to the by-now almost paralyzed lady, as I yanked on Lizzy's collar and leash and held on to her for dear life.

"She is not going to kill me, is she," was the horrified whisper from the affected lady.

I looked at 4 month old Lizzy, all legs, small body, cutely compacted face of a boxer, which now had a smile from ear to ear, with tongue panting and licking the upper lip, in anticipation of contact with human skin, straining at the leash to commence playing. And I glanced at the 5 foot 5 inch lady, stoutly built, and towering 4 feet above Lizzy. Not a fair match I thought, totally one-sided!

"This piece of fur-ball . . . . nah . . . . she is not gonna 'kill' you." I tried hard not to laugh!

I swore after this never to take the stairs and bump into mortally afraid neighbors! But our elevator had a peculiar habit. It refused to work when the electricity was out and the building was on generator supply! So the stairs it was, on these occasions, which were quite a few since our city was rather notorious for unscheduled power shut downs with irritating regularity.

I was always wary when I took Lizzy downstairs by stairs. Initially, for sometime after this harrowing episode, I literally crept down the stairs, holding Lizzy close to me. After a while, with no further close encounters of the fourth kind with any humans, I released my death hold on Lizzy's collar. Lizzy's joy knew no bounds! She would tug once, realize the leash was loose, and then tear down the stairs, like the devils of hell were chasing her! At each floor, she would stop.

"Woof woof!"

"Lizzy, I am coming! Stop making a racket!" As if the fur-ball could try and understand me!

"Lizzy!" I yelped, as I cannoned into a waiting pup in the second floor.

"Woof!" and she raced down again.

"God! Would you stop it already!"

This time I approached the first floor lobby cautiously, and sure enough she was waiting for me at the bend! Ploughing into her was getting to be a game to Lizzy now!

"Woof!" and she was off again. She raced into the garden, sniffing every object on the ground and even tasting some, until she realized that I was hot on her heels.

"Lizzy stop!"

Lizzy was obedient if nothing else! She obeyed commands and accepted them as part of her life. She understood and picked up the meaning of all our instructions very quickly, and we actually had never imparted any formal training to her. She was a natural. Even on the roads, I had drilled into her that she should come onto one side in case there was traffic. She would. But over the months, with so many people taking her for walks, not the least of them the servant maids, she tended to forget the instructions, at the most inappropriate times!

In the early days, she would jump down the last few steps of the stair-case and then gambol down into the garden within the apartment complex. This was another one of her favorite spots. Racing across the narrow lawn on either side of the footpath, leading to the car garage, at supersonic speeds, was the crowning glory of the day for her. She would take the bends and leap onto the other side at the same speed, without breaking a gallop or hitting anything there. Inevitably, some of the smaller plants perished at her expense, but the garden was none the worse for it, due to the tender nurturing by the apartment gardener. She still does that and its always a pleasure to see the way she tucks her hind legs in to make her body small, but never sacrificing the speed of travel! I don't stop her or caution her, because she obviously knows her limits. Even her halts are flawless!

I am always apprehensive that one or the other flat owners will object. But the utter joy and freedom that Lizzy experiences and rejoices in, makes me want to defy the world, just so that she can enjoy those few moments of total unrestricted pleasure at being free, after the confinement in the apartment.

I keep thinking that as humans, can we not just appreciate the freedom that another living being desires and revels in, without objecting to it, just because it's a 'dog'? Sadly, very few people share my enthusiasm. I have been reprimanded, sometimes with dire legal consequences, by other humans, upon seeing Lizzy not tied onto a leash and being held by a human.

It goes without saying that the plastic bottles and other destructibles, left lying around by the security staff, took quite a beating and if any were empty, Lizzy would promptly cart it over to the house, as part of her booty collection! No amount of cajoling to drop the plastic bottle, would have any effect on her. Severe remonstration would cause her to drop it, but then she would be sulking for the next half hour, and frankly, it wasn't worth that.

Another of her hot favorites was the tender coconut shell. She carts it along during the walks when she finds them discarded on the road. The early morning walkers have all been introduced to this novel site of a dog holding a big coconut shell in its mouth for the entire duration of the walk! She will drag on her leash the moment she discovers one on the road, and put her foreleg on it, laying claim to it! No amount of cajoling will drag her away from it. Small coconuts were all right, if she caught it rightly, her teeth in the opening, but large shells do not sit on her jaw properly and I suffer pangs of sympathy for her labor!

From then on, I started to sternly order her to drop the big ones. She does it, albeit rather reluctantly, giving it longing glances all the while until it am out of sight. Once, I have actually dragged her with her face turned backwards for the full length of the road, till we reached a bend! Of course, the moment I completed a full walk and if I happened to come anywhere in that vicinity again, she has to drag herself to the coconut shell and look at me, tongue lolling . . . ." c'mon, its ok now right. I have completed the walk, now at least . . . . ??" I have to give in then! Who can resist a 2 feet brown mutt with lolling tongue, a roguish look in its eyes and panting in anticipation of playing with a huge 'ball'!

The branched twig of the coconut tree is another preferred item of play for Lizzy! Of course, for that she required a partner in crime . . . . me! She will latch onto the branch and bring it tantalizingly close to me, looking at me from the corner of her eyes, growling softly, as if to challenge me! I am expected to rise to the challenge suitably, pull on the stick with all my might, so as to almost dislodge it, but not take it out fully, for to yank it out of her jaws was to insult Lizzy and she will lick her lips sorrowfully in embarrassment! This could go on for a while, till I get bored of it, and then throw the stick as far as possible! Lizzy will race after the offending stick, growling all the way, and then grab it in mid-air triumphantly, proceeding to bring it back to me.

"Get lost Lizzy, I am so not throwing it again!"

"Woof! Grrr . . . ."

She will stand before me, rear end shaking in anticipation, demanding that I play ball!

This can continue till she sees or hears another creature moving. If it is another unknown dog, she will race down the pitch till the end of the apartment complex, making sure the dog was completely out of sight and range! But if it is a rat or a squirrel, she will not give up chase even to the extent of burrowing into the ditch to chase it!

"Lizzy stop! Don't jump across the gate! Lizzy!!!"

Lizzy jumped! I don't think she heard my cries at all! She was so caught up in the moment!

"Lizzy, do not enter the ditch! Lizzy!"

I was talking to her rump! I couldn't see her after that for about 5 secs. I then *heard* a plaintive cry!

"Lizzy! Is that you? Lizzy!" I screeched frantically, really worried now, for Lizzy basically never yelps in pain, never fusses.

"Security! Pl open the side gates!" I yelled, gesturing to the gate opposite where I was standing.

Before the gates were fully open, I dashed across to peer into the ditch adjoining our apartment. Yeah, there was the all familiar rump with the tail stump!

"Lizzy! You daft mutt!"

There was only a melancholic whine in response.

I giggled. She was not hurt, that was all that mattered.

"Lizzy, you can stay there for sometime till you realize that your body cannot fit into every passageway and crevice possible!"

I let her stew inside for a while. I know, cruel, but Lizzy needed a lesson or two in discipline and common sense and controlling impulses!

Animals are really God's creatures. Lizzy stayed there without much fuss! Of course, she could still smell me around and didn't get so frightened, trusting that I would do right by her! After a short while, the security guard and I dragged her backwards from the ditch, into which her rump was tightly wedged. Lizzy couldn't move the rear part of her body, although her head could turn around and she had plenty of breathing space inside the ditch. We had to remove the granite coverings of the ditch and clear away the muck inside so as to dislodge her hips and slowly move her out!

Lizzy was so overjoyed at being free that she made a beeline for my face and planted her forelegs on my shoulder to give my face a thorough wash with her tongue.

"Thank you, thank you, thank you . . . . ! Boy it was dark in there!" she seemed to say.

"Lizzy, learn to follow instructions and not dive headfirst into anything and everything!" I remonstrated sternly.

"Woof! Woof! I love you! Talk to the back" was all her panting face seemed to say, as she raced away from us, rounded the bend and ploughed into the apartment complex, with nary an ill-effect from her imprisonment just a while back!

# (8)

## *Baby-sitting!*

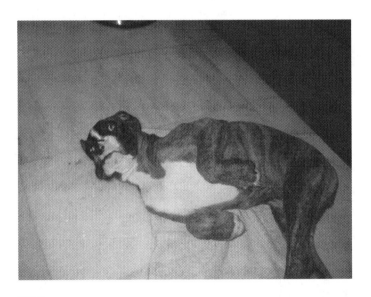

**W**hen Lizzy first came to us, we had no strategy in place as to how she would cope being left alone at home, when all of us were gone, for work or school. We had, clearly, not thought it through. We presumed that the pup would get the hang of it after some days! Immature of us obviously, because apparently, Lizzy had her own ideas on that score! So initially, abhishek stayed back from school, and kept Lizzy company, alternating with akhilesh. I had a part-time help those days, who would come in the morning and leave by mid-morning.

A week later, we decided that so many days leave from school is not likely to go down well with the school authorities! So it was arranged with the maid, that she would come in a little later, just as we were about to leave, and then stay back as late as possible, till the boys came back from school. In theory, that should have worked pretty well! It did for a few days, but then, as is *au naturale,* the maid started coming later and later and we had to leave Lizzy alone for some time, and of course, she called in sick quite a few days.

Leaving her on her own, even with the balcony left wide open for her to look around and bark at all things moving, did not go well with Lizzy! She was a people dog and she did not like being left alone, even for a short while. And she showed us her displeasure in many ways, with constant regularity! The bathroom door was always open for her to use it for peeing, but Lizzy insisted on making a mess all around the house in revenge! The bathroom was left spotless! Of course, the moment one of us came in, she would obediently run to the bathroom to relieve herself, the picture of submissiveness!

Then she took to destroying things! We came back home to see pens chewed up, slippers carefully kept at a higher place, ostensibly out of her reach, would be in layers! Even the wooden stand at the bottom of the huge settee, had been gnawed to retrieve the toy that had gone underneath . . . . some months ago! One by one, all things chewable or playable by Lizzy, had to be tucked away in safety, away from the eyes of the brat!

Since the kitchen was open, with no door, it was like an invitation to Lizzy! She rummaged through the dustbin before my maid could come and empty it! The maid entered the house to see a pile of rubbish strewn all over the kitchen and the living room floor . . . . and there was a nice waft lifting off it, like somebody had died in there a week ago! To add to her misery, Lizzy had considerately peed there too!

Lizzy thought everybody was having great fun, screaming at her and brandishing the broom at her, during clean-up time!

"Woof, woof! Bring it on!" she barked, adopting a crouching position, front legs down and rump in the air. She made a playful lunge at the broom for good measure, just to indicate, that she was definitely playing!

"You want to play is it? I am going to give you good now! Scat!" my maid shouted, in great angst, at all the extra work. She lifted the broom to land one on Lizzy's back, and Lizzy went berserk, thinking it was still a very nice game, although the tone of the maid's voice was changing in inflection that left Lizzy in some doubt.

"Get lost! Go play with your bone or something!"

"Woof, woof!"

"Ok, you asked for it." And as she lunged at Lizzy, she was totally unprepared for an aerial assault by Lizzy! Before she knew it, she was on the ground and the broom was being demolished by Lizzy!

So there was mayhem all around, with mounds of rubbish, some pee, and bits and pieces and powder of the broom, and of course, a smattering of drool from Lizzy, as seasoning! Since the maid was rather fond of dogs and especially so of Lizzy, whom she had been with from day one, she let Lizzy have her way, groaning and moaning as she burrowed her way through all the rubbish, shooing and scatting the little brat, now and then.

The moment she got through with the cleaning, I received a frantic call from her, detailing all the travails of the morning. I groaned inwardly, but what could one do. Such is the way of a dog left loose!

If we thought that was the last of it, we were all very sadly mistaken, because Lizzy had her own thoughts about that, and that did not bode well for us.

It was a nice cool morning, such as Bangalore was wont to experience almost every day, a decade ago. The sun was playing hide and seek with the clouds, and there was a gentle breeze billowing across the house. We left Lizzy enjoying the cool summer on the balcony, while we made our way out. She looked at us rather despondently, and then ran back to the balcony to see us off. I was left wondering which object in the house would face her wrath today, and how much I would have to shell out for that!

I got busy in hospital after that. About mid-afternoon, I got a harassed call from abhishek.

"Ma, guess what?" he started ominously. "You will never guess in a million years what Lizzy-the-great has done," he countered, hanging on to the phone in suspense.

"Ok spill it out. You are killing me here," I replied, my heart thudding.

"Just guess ma."

"Abhishek, I am gonna physically come there and wring your neck, if you don't spill the beans in a second!"

"Ok ok, chill ma." He waited for a further ten seconds.

"Abhishek!"

"Lizzy has torn the single sofa, and the hall is a total wreck, with sponge and cotton all over the place. She has also passed urine over the cotton in some places!"

I was too numb to reply right away. My foreboding in the morning panned out. I was so furious with Lizzy that I decided I was definitely going to wring her neck and feed her to the crows!

"I have already shouted at her and locked her up in the balcony."

I could hear Lizzy's plaintive cries in the background.

"Ma, there's cotton strewn all over the house, some in my room as well," my younger son chipped in.

Apparently, my maid had left early today, after finishing her work, before my sons could come back from school. Left with nothing else to do, Lizzy had decided to re-arrange the single sofa! And she had been merciless at that! The rexin covering was in tatters, the inner sponge was ripped apart, and the cotton, some of it still stuck to her mouth, was floating in her pee and creating a Halloween effect all over the living room! Although I had expected to see a disaster zone, this was way beyond comprehension! A rookie medical trainee could not have dissected a body more thoroughly!

"You are so grounded for life from the sofa, from the bed, from anything you are used to!" I yelled at Lizzy through the balcony door, into which she was still locked up.

"Woof, woof! Let me out first!" she yelped, apparently unfazed, behind a wooden door which was shut and through which, she knew, I could not reach!

While abhishek went off to sleep to prepare for the evening 3 hrs. of tuition, akhilesh proceeded to change and pack for his tuition, so I was left holding the broom and the pan! I looked longingly at the bed. If I could just rest my head for a while, I thought to myself. But the mess here beckoned, and I could not rest in peace with such a slummed out area in my house!

I could not salvage much. A few large pieces of sponge, some untorn rexin pieces, and a substantial amount of the cotton, was all I managed to set aside. I now had to look out for a sofa repair hawker, who would use all these bits and pieces and save me some money. The mangled sofa looked quite miserable, and I sighed, resigned to my fate of having to spend at least five grand on the darn thing! The flak I was going to receive from my husband, was something I didn't want to dwell upon!

Lizzy was still in the balcony, although her thunderous woofs had reduced to pitiful whines now. I decided to let her stew there for some more time, as I took some well earned rest on the large settee. As I settled down comfortably, Lizzy suddenly let out a yell!

"Ma, enough, let her out now, poor thing," abhishek called out, walking out sleepily from his room.

"I am not letting her into the living room," I retorted.

"Ok, I will let her in then."

Lizzy darted out from the balcony like a bullet from a rifle! She never liked being away from me for any length of time. Unless I sit with her in the balcony, she did not have the habit of sitting there for more than 3-5 minutes. So being in there for like an hour, was killing her and freedom was like a whole new life for her!

She instantly jumped onto me, and licked me all over, all past misdemeanors forgotten!

"Lizzy get offa me! You are not my most favorite living being right now!" I yelled, pushing her off me.

Lizzy stopped licking and looked at me sideways. She sniffed the air to gauge how serious I was and if there was going to be any severe repercussions. Deciding things were too confusing, she got off me, and settled down at my son's feet, as he was sipping tea. I pointedly ignored her side-long glances to see if I had cooled off.

"Ma, give her a break. Its not like she deliberately does these things to harass you!"

"I am really not in a forgiving mood right now, and I am so dreading your father's reaction to it!" I moaned softly.

"Get it repaired before he comes"

"Yeah, like the repair guy is just hanging outside the house waiting for me to call him!"

I looked at Lizzy morosely. She thumped her 'tail', lifted her head slightly, and slyly extended her fore paws towards me. She just needed any sign to jump all over me. She had not officially greeted me on my return, and in her doggy mind, something was pending and needed rectification urgently! I sighed in resignation. Fate cannot be argued with.

"Why can't you just be a normal dog waiting for us to come back home and watching the sights outside till we return?" I asked her softly, extending my hand towards her. That was a rhetorical question more to Him than to Lizzy. But that did not perturb Lizzy in the least! She saw her moment and seized it fully! She jumped square onto my tummy and squatted there till she had thoroughly licked every portion of my exposed face! It would not have stopped there had I not enveloped her in my arms and crushed her to me, digging my face into her soft face, as I moaned my sorrows to her! She kept wriggling to gain access to my face again, but I just held her tight.

"Ok ok, you guys! Get a room!" my son snorted disgustedly.

"Lizzy, come lets go to the bedroom!" I grinned, baiting my son.

"Ma, that's disgusting!"

"You have a dirty mind!" I retorted.

"Yeah, right. You guys better behave till I come back." He had to give a last parting short, as he walked out of the door to leave for his tuition.

Lizzy was none the worse for the ordeal she had put us through. She promptly settled down to bask in my presence and while away the time, till such time that she heard a dog outside the house and felt she has to bark to let the dog know she was there to protect her human family.

I entrusted my maid to look for the hawker to repair the settee. She would be able to hear him go in the mornings when she was home doing the chores. It took a while for her to catch hold of him as there was a mis-match of timings. But catch hold of him she did finally. He looked at the settee and quoted a pretty nominal price for all the damage and I thankfully got the settee repaired.

But it did not happen in time for my husband to comment on the damage!

"My God! You have no license where the dog is concerned! You and the dog have gone berserk! This settee will never be the same, thanks to your dog! Disgusting!" he raged. "There will be serious consequences if I see that dog on the settee henceforth!"

I sat through it all mutely, because anything I said then would have blown into a full scale war! He refused to acknowledge Lizzy after that, considering her a menace from hell! Lizzy, for her part, didn't feel there was any less love for him, than before. She always greeted him deliriously whenever he came home, not minding a bit that he shoved her aside!

# (9)

*My baby is growing up . . . . !*

Lizzy was the quintessential Jack-in-the-box or more aptly, Jill-in-the-box! She loved life, humans and everything that was associated with these two aspects and her joie-de-vivre was very contagious. I have so often come back home after a tired day's work with a gigantic migrainous headache but her enthusiastic greetings and boisterous love, never failed to put a smile on my face, a thrill in my heart, and the disappearance of my headache.

She brought a refreshing change to the monotony of our evenings. There was always something happening with Lizzy around, and she would drag us all back to the fun in life with her on-the-move attitude to life.

I had long ago decided that if and when I had a dog, I would not get puppies out of her. I did not approve of breeding just for the sake of getting puppies for I did not want to wonder about the fate of the poor pups, whether they had gone into good homes and if their human owners were treating them like another member of their family or just a 'dog' to be tied and forgotten outside and left to its own devices to amuse itself.

I had consulted several veterinary doctors whether female dogs underwent any psychological disturbances if they were denied mating and bearing of pups, and I had received an almost universal response that there was no such problem with animals.

So by the time Lizzy was approaching 8-9 months of age, I decided to spay her. I was advised by the vet that spaying them earlier, before the onset of their first menstrual cycle, was medically safer for them, as it prevented cancer of the reproductive system later in life.

So when Lizzy turned 8 ½ months, we decided it was time to do it. She was given a date for surgery and the pre-op preparations required just one day.

On the scheduled day, Lizzy was kept on empty stomach overnight, which didn't bother her at all I am sure! In fact, it must have pleased her no end that she did not have to endure another feeding session!

It was a fine December morning, in fact, X'mas day. The weather was nippy but not cold, and Lizzy bounded into the car with the same joyous abandon, that she always did!

The hospital was a short distance, and we were early, in fact, before time. The surgery was scheduled for 9.30 am. The doctor arrived at 9 am. By this time, Lizzy was not too happy with her surroundings! She could get all the smells associated with an animal hospital, and her nose was twitching in anxiety. Whatever we had got her here for could not be good for her peace of mind, she decided. I had still not taken her out of the car.

The orderly came out to start an Intra-venous line for her. I held her on my lap inside the car on the back seat, and crooned softly while he deftly inserted the line without any trouble. Lizzy was absolutely still. He injected the pre-anesthetic medication into the IV.

"She will become drowsy in a while. We will wheel her into the Operation theatre then," he said.

"You will be taking her in or shall I?"

Being a doctor, I was still showing all the signs of apprehension that was typical of a laymen! But that was to be expected since I considered Lizzy as my baby girl!

He smiled, used to anxious 'parents'!

"I'll take her in. Let her doze off a bit."

I sat on the back seat with Lizzy. She rested her head on my lap, already feeling the effects of the IV and looked up at me, trustingly, drowsily. I patted her head on my lap and crooned softly.

"Sleep off baby. You'll be good and ready to come home in one hour."

Soon her head felt heavy on my lap. I gestured to the orderly and he gently lifted up Lizzy in his arms and carried her into the hospital. I was so glad that such care and tenderness was being shown, because in our country, animals are below second or even third class citizens! CESSNA hospital, where the surgery was conducted is still a top notch hospital for animal care, with the doctors there very considerate and caring to the animals.

The next two hours were quite the longest I have had to face in living memory! Lizzy was such an essential part of our lives, such an integral part, another loving soul to be looked after, that it was unthinkable to be without her loving, jumpy presence. Abhishek called up within an hour to find out how things were. He knew how fretful I would be.

"She's in. The surgery should take only 45 minutes, and some more time for recovery. So she should be out in an hour." I replied softly, keeping my fingers crossed.

"Ok, call me if needed."

"Son, I need you both to come down when I reach the gates, so as to help me lift Lizzy up into the house from the car."

"Yeah, ok. Call when you leave the hospital."

Since it was Christmas, and a holiday, both my sons were at home.

I tried reading a storybook, while sitting snugly inside the car. It was turning out to be a warm day, but I could still feel a shiver down my spine on and off. I would read a page and then my thoughts would wander to the joie-de-vivre that Lizzy always exhibited. I would pull my thoughts back to the book at hand. Finally, I shrugged off the gloomy feelings and stepped outside the car to inhale the cool December air.

I trudged inside the reception area and the same attender grinned at my worried face. I passed my time looking at all the items on display for all the four-legged pets. Such attractive logos and packaging would tempt the worst scrooge to buy something for their pooch!

I decided to go back to my book. It was mid-morning now and I liked the idea of completing the story I had started! I had just turned two pages, when the attender came out to inform me to keep the car doors open, since they were bringing Lizzy out. I jumped out and yanked the rear door open, adjusted the bedspread neatly on the seat, and waited to see my baby!

Two assistants carried Lizzy aloft in their arms and then gently placed her horizontally on the seat. Lizzy was groggy still but even then she made a vain attempt to stand up!

"Lie back, Lizzy," I crooned to her softly.

Lizzy settled down with a sigh. She was reassured by my voice. All this while, she had heard only strangers bark instructions. Now she was back in her world with me.

Her tongue was out still and I put that back inside, manually. She didn't like it! She probably thought it was the surgeons doing all those rotten invasive things to her respiratory system again. So she attempted to get up again. I patted her back.

The attenders were watching all this in amusement!

"You can come inside now and pay the bill. We will look after her in here," one of them commented.

"Yes madam. Come with me." The other said, obligingly.

I went inside with him and completed all the formalities. I also spoke to the chief veterinarian surgeon.

"No problems?" I asked gingerly.

"No. It all went smoothly. I have written down a few antibiotics and pain-killers for the next 5 days. She should be fully conscious by evening. Don't give her any heavy food till tomorrow. She will vomit due to the anesthetic effect."

"So, what should I give her? Milk? Eggs? Porridge?"

"Give her milk if she has or a half-boiled egg." the vet instructed. "Start the medicines in the afternoon, since we have given her a first dose via the intra-venous line."

I tipped the attender outside for his help, wrapped Lizzy up inside a bed sheet securely, and got into the driver's seat to proceed home.

"Son, I will be home in 10 minutes. You come down. Leave the front door wide open. Tell akhilesh to arrange Lizzy's bed in the living room." I instructed abhishek.

I drove slowly so as to not to jerk Lizzy and cause her pain at the operated site. Abhishek was waiting near the apartment gates when I reached there in 10 minutes. I slowly parked the car close to the gates. We opened the rear doors. Abhishek took the head end of Lizzy along with the bed sheet, while I stepped inside the car and lifted Lizzy up from her rear side. Lizzy stirred violently and jerked her head!

"Slow down baby, sleep now," I crooned.

We then slowly made our way out of the car, leaving the doors open. I called softly to the security guard at the gates and requested him to shut the car doors and lock the car. He handed the keys to me after locking the car and abhishek and I made our way up to the elevators. The security guard looked aghast at the huge bandage on Lizzy's midriff!

We gingerly maneuvered the doors of the elevator. Lizzy's body was totally lax now and she was pretty long horizontally, and pretty heavy! It was one of those old time elevators, where the steel doors had to be manually pulled shut and did not automatically close. So I had to call the security guard to close the doors while we held Lizzy inside. He came to the doors and still had his mouth open in shock!

Akhilesh was waiting at the door as we exited the elevator. He helpfully opened the elevator doors for us and we carefully got Lizzy out. He had placed Lizzy's bed in the living room so that she need never be alone as we went about our tasks for the day.

We placed Lizzy gently on her bed. She jerked awake suddenly and gave a wild look at us! She made a feral attempt at biting the bandage on her midriff!

"Lizzy no!"I yelled, pushing her head back firmly on the bed.

In her half dazed status, Lizzy, for the first and probably the last time in her life, bit my hand that pushed her head! She had a half-crazed look on her face that said "don't mess with me!" This was a wild, untamed Lizzy that I had never encountered and it made me uncomfortable for days, and also brought home the truth, that for all her love and domestication, Lizzy was, at base level, an animal!

To say I was startled was putting it mildly! Lizzy was such an affectionate, docile living being and so devoted to me that I could never fathom such an action on her part. Of course, none of us held that against her, for we knew the semi-conscious state she was in, not knowing what she was doing or the consequences of her action.

For her part, Lizzy dozed off after that attempt at tasting my hand! If she had realized that she had tried taking a bite off her beloved mistress' hand, Lizzy would have definitely gone into depression . . . . if there was anything like that in the doggie world!

We were all, most of the time, huddled around her bed. I ate my lunch sitting on the floor next to Lizzy, so that she would always feel our presence and never feel left out. She slept for a solid 4 hours after her surgery, wincing now and then in pain from the surgical wound.

When she did wake up, it was a turbulent episode! We were all watching TV, which was at a low volume, so as to not to disturb Lizzy, and none of us saw or heard any movement. She just swung her face and elevated her entire torso in one go! She was as bemused as the rest of us on seeing herself up and swaying!

We rushed to her side to help her steady herself. She refused to accept our help, yelping in pain on taking her first step forward.

"Oh poor baby. Come here sweetheart," I said, putting my arms around her, almost in tears myself.

She whined and flopped onto my lap wondering what had happened to her gait!

"Its ok darling. You'll be alright."

"Why don't you give her a pain-killer, ma."

"She has already received an injectable one after the surgery, son. I need to repeat that only in the evening."

"Cant you give her a small dose now, to reduce her pain?" my younger son insisted.

"She will have vomiting and gastric upset, if I repeat it so soon, especially since she has not eaten anything and is on empty stomach."

The subject in question had, in the meantime, burrowed into my lap, curling up in a fetal position, unperturbed and oblivious to all the attention. But hers was a rather disturbed sleep after that. Probably the pain-killer was wearing off and she felt something gnawing at her hip.

"Ok sweetheart, I will give you an analgesic to ease you out," I said softly, not used to seeing Lizzy bothered by pain so much. Lizzy usually was very nonchalant about any injury or hurt, and even if there was an out pouring of blood, she would calmly lick the wound, but never whine or ask for attention. So her distress at this point, obviously meant she was in considerable pain.

I fed her a half-boiled egg, the kind she liked, where the yellow or the yolk portion was still liquid enough to lick it up. She thoroughly enjoyed that and dozed again. I nudged her gently to see if she would take some warm milk. Surprisingly she made an attempt to lap that up as well, although she didn't quite finish it. After that, I did give her a half-strength of an analgesic to ease the pain.

We lifted Lizzy bodily en mass with her mattress and shifted her to the bedroom so that she could be with me for the afternoon as we both snoozed! Lizzy was mighty surprised to see herself suddenly elevated and travelling across mid-air! She sniffed the air expectantly, decided that it was all her loved ones, again acting crazy as usual, sighed deeply and flopped back to sleep!

"Her majesty!" abhishek snorted derisively.

"Cant get up and help us out?!" akhilesh countered.

I smiled lovingly at the fur-ball stretched luxuriously on her bed. Lizzy really knew how to soak it in! She had started to expect all the good things in life to happen to her! I kept her as close to my cot as possible so that she could feel my presence and be re-assured. Giving a contented sigh, I too curled up snugly into my blanket and drifted into sleep.

Okay, I cannot be dreaming that so vividly, I thought to myself, half asleep, a low whine ringing in my ears. I brushed it aside again, and pulled the blanket over my ears.

There it was again, a low plaintive cry for attention!

"Lizzy!" I jerked up awake thinking the worst possible scenario.

But Lizzy was squatting on her bed, looking up at me expectantly, her soft brown eyes gazing up at me, hypnotically

"Woof." Lizzy replied in a low voice, and then yelped in pain as the strain pulled all the operation stitches.

"Ok, ok. I cant be coming down to keep you company, so obviously you want to force your way into my bed."

She whined again.

"My God! You really demand to be fussed, don't you."

I had not the faintest idea how I was going to lift Lizzy up onto my bed. But it seemed like she was not going to let me hear the end of it! So up she had to come.

Lizzy was sitting on her haunches waiting to be pulled up. Its like she was saying to me "get up and get the rest of me on to your bed! You don't have to be so comfortable there all by yourself!"

I groaned as I lifted the blanket off my warm body.

Lizzy licked her lips eagerly! She just liked the idea of sleeping close to me, and it would not have mattered to her had I just come down and slept with her on her mattress. It was not the comfort of the bed she was looking at but the proximity of her mistress. It was pure love.

I lifted her front legs onto the bed and slowly elevated her rear end en mass onto the bed, so as to not to disturb the operated area. She flopped there, close to the edge and looked at me with those soulful eyes!

"Yeah, yeah, I am coming!" I replied.

I crept into my side of the bed and placed the blanket on both of us. Lizzy gave a huge sigh and closed her eyes contently.

And that's how my sons found us later in the evening, as they quietly opened the door to see what was going on inside, since things were a mite too quiet and peaceful! I was already up by then and tenderly passing my hand over Lizzy's head. She was still sleeping, contently. On hearing the door open, she first opened one eye, then the other, stretched herself languidly, then squeaked in pain, startled to find that her mid-riff was sending in twinges of agony! She licked her lips in embarrassment, then looked up happily to see the rest of her family around, fussing over her and cooing over her.

I decided to take her for short walk outside, just to get her out of the house and into the fresh air outside.

"Come Lizzy, walk," I called out tantalizingly.

Lizzy came to the edge of the bed and then looked up expectantly. She pawed the edge and whined plaintively, eyeing the floor in dread, knowing that if she jumped she would probably feel pain in the mid-riff. She sat down on her haunches and waited patiently.

"Ok, ok," I laughed. "We will pick up her majesty and deposit her on the ground."

With her feet firmly on terra firma, Lizzy heaved a sigh of relief. She slowly took a few steps forward, and immediately whipped her head to the operated site, trying to get at the bandage and lick the offending area, as it tugged at her pain nerves.

"No Lizzy, leave that alone. Walk slowly, it doesn't matter," I remonstrated, fearing she would pull the bandage out and open the wound.

Lizzy reluctantly shifted her head away from her mid-riff and started moving forward, but she would keep turning her head side wards as the tinges of pain hit her.

I decided to cover up the huge bandage with one of my sons' old T-shirts. So I pulled the neck of the T-shirt over Lizzy's head and squeezed her fore limbs into the arms of the T-shirt. It was a navy blue one with the head of a polar bear on the front, as an appliqué design. Lizzy looked comical but at least, it covered that gigantic bandage!

Lizzy did not approve of it! She tried her best to wriggle out of it, but the T-shirt fit snugly, and would not submit to her fidgeting. With a huge sigh of resignation, and a pitiful look at me from the corner of her eye, she trudged forward towards the door.

"Eeks!" my sons shrieked as they saw Lizzy coming out in a jumper suit!

"Ma, you cannot, absolutely cannot take her out in this state!"

"She is an insult to this household!" my younger son claimed dramatically.

"Ma, the other dogs will tease her and she will die of shame!" this from my elder son, who notoriously wears his pants practically on his groin, which so makes me cringe!

"Aw, put a lid on it you two! Its not like she's out for a ramp walk. This is practical and it covers that obnoxiously huge bandage!"

"Ma, she could virtually start working in a circus! You got to do better than this, please!"

"Well, this is the best I got. So live with it!" I snapped back.

So Lizzy and I went for our usual walks without flinching. But when it was the turn of my sons to take her out in the evenings . . . . oh boy, the fuss they made! I am sure even Lizzy did not really mind it that much, but my sons were wishing the earth would swallow them each time they made their way out with Lizzy in that T-shirt! They took to leaving the house when it was dark outside so that none of their friends in the neighborhood would recognize them! This went on for quite a while till one of their friends did recognize them and started guffawing at the sight of Lizzy!

That was the final straw that broke the camel's back! They refused to be seen out with Lizzy in that 'contraption' as they called it! So I had to take the T-shirt out and reduce the size of the bandage, although the operated site with its hair shaved off was pretty much obvious even at night times, as it contrasted with the dark fur on Lizzy's back!

Lizzy on her part, kept trying to gnaw at the loose ends of the T-shirt as it fell down from her mid-riff, but submitted to fate when her short jaws could not quite get a hold of the ends! She trotted along her walks primly and for once there were no mishaps even when we sighted cats or squirrels along the way.

The wound healed well. I had to clean it each day with antiseptic solution and put a tight plaster on it and bandage it for a couple of days so that Lizzy wouldn't tear the plaster away. Of course, I decreased the size of the bandage and it did not look so horrific ever again! After 5-6 days, the wound developed a nice scab and I stopped dressing it. The bandage came off, and another couple of days later, the plaster was not required either.

But the hair removed from that area was mighty slow in growing back and invited a lot of comments, quite a few of them from my darling husband!

"Even when I do brain surgery, I don't shave off so much hair. This looks so disfiguring!" he remarked disdainfully.

"Just ignore it for a couple of weeks and it will grow back" I replied, hoping to settle the matter.

"A couple of weeks! My God! We have to bear this god-awful sight for a couple of weeks!"

"Pa, don't get ma started about the disfiguring or else she will put the T-shirt on back!" my sons chorused enthusiastically.

I glowered at them. Here I was trying to diffuse a flammable situation and they were certainly not helping matters.

"Oh God! Not the T-shirt!" he groaned.

"Ok ok. Have we all had enough fun at my expense or is there more to come? Can we get on with our lives please?" I retorted back, exasperatedly.

Lizzy slept through the whole tirade!

She recovered beautifully after that, by leaps and bounds. The wound healed completely with a small scar. The hair grew back and one could not even make out that she had had that surgery. Thankfully there were no post-op complications. As a doctor, I had seen so many surgeries go awry and my experience with animals also made me a cynic, since they were not the most obedient of patients and invariably tore their bandages out, leading to secondary infection and loss of suture, which led to opening of the surgical wound. As each day passed, and I could see the surgical wound closing, it was very heartening. I did take Lizzy to the vet for a review and he whole-heartedly voiced his approval at the situation. Only one suture had to be removed and then she was on a home run.

Lizzy suffered no ill-effects of the spaying. The vet had warned us that her incontinence, or inability to hold her urine, would increase. But the Lizzy we knew did not change! Her urgency to pass urine was the same, no less no more! We had all gotten used to it by now and we followed a protocol like clockwork!

Lizzy had the same merry, jumpy, boisterous attitude as always and that has not changed to this day!

# (10)

## *Doggy acquaintances*

By this time, there were many dog owners trotting alongside their dogs for a routine morning walk. Of course, there were more of those who believed in just getting their pooches to do the big job, following which they would promptly scamper back home. But Lizzy and I made many friends along the way.

Our very first four-legged friend was Scotty! He was a beautiful golden Labrador, a hulking, gorgeous specimen of prime dog-hood! He was ever so friendly, like most Labradors are wont to be. When we met him, he was just over a year old, and decided, at first sight, that Lizzy was his eternal soulmate! He was so smitten by her that he had that moon-struck look on his face whenever he chanced upon her!

Scotty had to stand up to his full regal height and then wag his tail nineteen to the dozen, craning his neck high to add to his full height, so as to show Lizzy what a dynamic and handsome catch he was! Lizzy was not too impressed. Her main concern was to play! And play rough! And titillate! She would go up to a tightly leashed scotty, look him in the eye, and give a low growl to entice him to play. Scotty would go berserk! Since he barely paid attention to the instructions of his owners, Scotty perforce, had to be kept leashed at all times outside the house, although he enjoyed total freedom inside their house.

His owners were a middle-aged north-Indian business couple who, the first time I met them, were out for the walk with their daughter. They lived just two streets away, in a rented independent house, which had a large driveway. Many a time have Lizzy and Scotty romped vigorously on the driveway, with delighted devoted onlookers like us!

Fortunately, Scotty's owners were just as devoted to dogs as I was, which was a refreshing change, after the neglect and bohemian attitude of most dog owners. Lizzy for her part, finally discovered she could play rough with another living being, without too many yelps and screams and curses! Scotty was a perfect gentleman and believed in letting the lady have her way!

"Lizzy down. No no, Lizzy down. No jumping! Lizzy!" Scotty's owners. If there was one thing that everybody was mortally afraid of was Lizzy's leaping antics! Lizzy had to leap up to try and lick everybody's faces and being middle-aged does put you in a very defenseless position. One can't leap out of harm's way in time to avoid a mishap, with a living being like Lizzy's nimble-footedness.

"Aw, ouch! That hurt Lizzy!" he groaned, clutching his ample abdomen in agony, as one of Lizzy's high jumps landed bang on his mid-riff.

"You will have to do something about her jumping, please," he said, moaning in agony, all the while hoping I didn't feel bad about a complaint regarding the apple of my eye.

"I am so sorry. Lizzy! Stop jumping!"

Lizzy, as was usual, was blissfully unaware of the chaos she had just created, just cringing enough to show she had registered my stern voice in her doggy brain!

She turned her attention to Scotty.

"Hmpf, thank God, there is at least somebody sane in this world who actually knows how to play and not scream all the time!" Lizzy seemed to say, as she gave just one backward glance at all of us lesser mortals! Then she launched her attack on an unsuspecting Scotty!

She jumped up at him, pinned him down on the ground, giving low growls all the while, clutching the front end of his body with her two front legs. Scotty lapped up all the attention!

"Woof! Woof, woof, woof!" Scotty replied, gazing up happily at Lizzy, atop him.

"I think we should take this up on our driveway, instead of the street, where the traffic is a hindrance,"

Scotty's owners remarked. We had met up during the evening walk closer to their house.

Scotty agreed wholeheartedly!

Lizzy wanted to get ahead of everybody. She kept tugging on her leash. She had to be the lead of the pack. No other animal could get ahead of her in a walk. She was slightly more considerate towards humans! The moment Scotty got a tad to the fore, Lizzy would pull me all the way up front! This went on all the way till Scotty's house.

En route we did battle the occasional cat, which leaped onto a wall and then onto a roof, which Lizzy had no means of following, although she did make some attempts at scaling the wall, then a large squirrel, which scampered away to the highest branch on the tree, in response to which Lizzy tried to best the Olympic pole vault, but sadly fell short!

The locality's large rat or the bandicoot, popped up from the drain near their house, and promptly scurried right back inside, upon finding Lizzy's snout right on its face, and her jaws snapping at him desperately! Scotty trotted along, merrily, with a happy grin on his large face, tongue lolling side wards trying to keep pace with Lizzy's antics, blissfully unaware of her frantic efforts to rid the world of vermin! When Lizzy was around, that was Scotty's whole world for the time being, nothing else mattered!

I removed Lizzy's leash and she dashed across their drive in gay abandon! To get such free space after the confines of our apartment complex, was like a football field for her! Scotty nearly tripped over his owner's feet as they attempted to free him of his collar! He anxiously looked up at their faces. "Hurry up already! Lizzy is getting away! Time is of the essence!" he seemed to say!

He charged after Lizzy! "Woof, woof!" he roared into her ears.

In response, Lizzy snapped at him. She did not approve of male dogs getting so close! Scotty, as was his wont, started sniffing and licking Lizzy. Lizzy told him exactly what she thought of his juvenile behavior!

"Grrrrrrrr . . . . !" she snapped. She nipped him trying to get his tender nose, but Scotty just escaped in time. And then she raced across the drive, Scotty chasing her round and round! This went on for a while. In the meantime, the adults watched all this romping around fondly, catching up on the latest gossip of the neighborhood. Scotty, being the heavier of the two, flopped down after some time, exhausted in trying to keep pace with Lizzy's frolics. He looked up at her adoringly, panting like his tongue would drop out!

"Woof, woof! C'mon, play some more, you loser! Is that all you got?" Lizzy seemed to say, darting in and out, in front of him.

"Aw, sit down next to me girl. Feel the breeze. Can't you just take a break for a minute?" he groaned back. Scotty could not manage to gallop for long due to his weight.

Lizzy dashed in front of his face tantalizingly. She was a lissome lady and could run circles around anybody for hours and look none the worse for it. In fact, we think Lizzy considers it below her dignity to stop running or reducing her hyper-activity when her fellow humans can do more!

She put her front paws in front of his face, tushy up in the air, and growled at his face.

All Scotty could do in response, was to pant back at her!

"I think they need some water and we need some snacks!" remarked Scotty's owner delightedly. Only Scotty agreed readily with him! Lizzy was sorely disappointed that the game did not continue but had to be taken inside the house.

While Scotty replenished his energies lapping up cold water, Lizzy and I made our way out. I had two sons waiting back at home and I knew I would already be hearing no end about my coming back late! Lizzy gave one last longing look at the drive, where she could run and gallop at top speeds, and at Scotty inside the house, woofed at him seeking a response, and then resolutely turned back to accompany me. Scotty didn't lift his head from the bowl of water!

In a short while, Scotty's owners established a retail shop close to our apartment complex. So every evening, whenever I had to take Lizzy for a walk, we would stop by at the shop, where Scotty would be tied to the door, since he was wont to wander out of the area and not heed to commands. Scotty and Lizzy got to chase each other for a considerable amount of time that we spent there. It was a done deed! Then Scotty would stop in resignation, lap up water and look forlornly at Lizzy while she roamed around freely inside the compound, chasing rats, and cockroaches, and grasshoppers, even trying to taste a couple, if by chance they scurried close to her inquisitive nose!

Lizzy always heeded commands, and 'drop it' was a command often used to get her to spit out the offending item, however tasty it seemed to her! Lizzy immediately responded because she did not like being in the 'doghouse'! Another major positive character was her dis-inclination to leave me out of her sight! So she would never roam far enough to keep me away from her field of vision, and I could always call her back, or just whistle, in case she happened to wander outside the gates. She would straight away, drop anything at task and race back to me, to check if everything was ok here! She obviously thought that the call was a cry for help and she, the savior!

Every Sunday, when I took Lizzy for her morning walk, she met Scotty at his home and they tired themselves out for a good 45 minutes. This had become a routine for us now. Lizzy knew the street leading to his house very well, and would try and drag me along that street each morning! Of course, on working days, her morning walks could not mean meeting Scotty, since I would get late for work. But Sundays were always Scotty days and so were most evenings.

Till the time Scotty and his owners moved away!

That was quite a let down, since their new residence was nearly thrice the distance and there was no way that we would, even by chance, meet up with Scotty on our regular morning walks. We did try and meet with Scotty in the evenings when he would come to the shop but slowly even that stopped, when it became too strenuous for the lady to get Scotty all the way over, by walk, from her house so far away.

There was this one time that Scotty came to stay with us for 2-3 days. Scotty's owners were leaving for a distant place in the north of India, Rajasthan to be precise, and Scotty could not be left with just anybody and all the holiday homes for dogs were very expensive in those days, and pretty unknown, as to the kind of care they would give. So they requested me and I readily agreed.

This was not the first time I was looking after a pet for a friend. Back in the old days, when we didn't have Lizzy, I had been pretty busy looking after so many dogs, as my friends went on holidays. There was a boxer just like Lizzy, a male one named Pongo, who started my love affair with boxers. He was a delightful dog, not so hyper-active like Lizzy, but just as loving and affectionate.

Then there were these two Labrador 'pups', a golden male dog 9 months of age, and a jet black female, 7 months of age, aptly named 'Carbon'! Even at that age, they were not properly potty trained which was the only black mark against them, having to clean up the urine time and time again. Otherwise, they were gorgeous and loving and completely smitten with the human race!

So Scotty came over one fine Sunday afternoon. Of course, the moment he saw Lizzy, he forgot his owners! They could be gone to Mars for all he cared! He and Lizzy raced around our flat and barked out from the balcony to announce to all the other dogs!

"I am here! Oh I am so happy to be with my sweetheart! Could I be any more happier!" he roared to all the neighborhood dogs and anybody else who understood the various barks and yelps and growls!

"Grrrrrrrrrrrrr . . . ." Lizzy suddenly warned.

I stopped my conversation with the owners mid-way as I raced outside to see what was amiss. Lizzy was standing guard next to her bowl of freshly cooked chicken and Scotty was peering in to see what that delectable smell was.

It was the gourmet meal Lizzy got every Sunday, and she had no intention of sharing it with anybody, boy friend or no boy friend!

Scotty had never been given non-veg before and he instinctively knew that that enticing smell had to mean something tasty. So he just stood there, wagging his tail, not taking his eyes off the bowl of chicken, and occasionally looking up at Lizzy. Lizzy for her part, just stood there, next to her bowl, hair on her back standing straight, not blinking, uttering low-throated growls in stark warning! Face-off!

"Scotty, please come back," I beseeched in a low voice, desperately trying to diffuse the situation. Any stimulus could now aggravate Lizzy, who had no intention of backing off, when it concerned meat. Scotty too, I was sure, would not let go if he got close to the bowl. I did not want a vicious fight on my hands, especially when Scotty was being dropped off!

Seeing my tense demeanor, the owners shouted at Scotty to come back and slowly went up to him, tied the leash on him and pulled him back!

Lizzy was still growling softly, her lips bared in a fierce snarl! Her stance next to her bowl clearly implied "Don't mess with me!"

With Scotty out of the area, Lizzy finished her bowl of chicken in peace and then sauntered back inside. She trotted up to Scotty and wagged her tail at him as if nothing had happened. Scotty too decided to let bygones be bygones.

# (11)

## *A party!*

Lizzy was going to be a year old on 17th April and I wanted to do something special for her.

"It's a dog, for Pete's sake! Why would you want to plan something for a fur-ball that doesn't understand the meaning of a good party . . . . getting drunk and high!" was my husband's sly comment.

"Hey, what a great idea! Let's call all the dogs in the neighborhood and celebrate!" akhilesh chipped in. Children are always so enthusiastic.

"Ok. Take leave from your outdoor activities and chaperone the dogs!" I countered to my younger son.

"Huh? C'mon, just leave them on the terrace and let them have a ball, ma!"

"Yeah right!" I snorted derisively. "If only life were that simple. We would have every individual from every flat in our apartment complex, storming into our house, to give us a peace of their mind, and bar our existence in this complex henceforth! You do remember how welcome the dogs are, right?"

"Ok ma. Then at least call a couple of dogs for company and have it inside the house. You could call scotty," Abhishek said thoughtfully. "He'll slobber all over the place enough to give the effect of 3 dogs!" he chirped, chuckling at the image.

"Let me think over it." I said, closing the matter for now. I knew the suggestions would be endless, but the help, in actual terms, zero, nada, zilch! My family did not believe in pitching in physically, only in spirit, and I didn't want to take on a herculean task on my own!

I had, of course, a plan afoot all along!

In fact, I had already set it into motion by ordering and getting a vanilla b'day cake from the local bakers the previous evening! It was a simple cake with minimal frosting on top. Lizzy liked vanilla flavor! Chocolate, of course, was toxic for dogs. I had brought it with me on my way back home last evening, and slyly smuggled it in, into the refrigerator. My sons did not believe in nosing around food sources!

I got up on the d-day, to find Lizzy helpfully snuggling on my feet, as a reminder that it was her special day and she, therefore, could not be berated! I reached out for her on the bed, and cuddled her warmly, showering kisses on the forehead . . . . and then quickly depositing her on the ground, for I knew what would happen to Lizzy's weak bladder if she got excited! And I did not want any soiling of my bed sheets!

She was a warm bundle of fur and was a delight to be held close on this a cold morning. Dogs have a higher body temperature than humans, but that apart, Lizzy, having cuddled up on my blanket for long time, had become even more warm, which had permeated every millimeter of her body, including the bare skin on the underside of her belly.

Lizzy was puzzled to find herself unceremoniously dumped on the cold ground, after a warm greeting! She stretched lazily and looked up at me, to give her obvious opinion at being shaken off the bed.

"Oh no Lizzy, you are not getting back on the bed again! B'day or no b'day. You have a perfectly warm, soft bed of your own, use that please!" I remonstrated, nudging her towards her bed in the corner. "Or you can accompany me to the kitchen," I offered helpfully.

She sighed and settled down comfortably on her bed!

Lizzy did not believe in losing her beauty sleep this early in the morning! I wished her a 'happy b'day', gave her one more tight hug and then proceeded to do my day's work. I, the human, had to face my responsibilities, one of which was getting food on the table for the rest of my family and attending work, quite in that order!

Her majesty came over to give me a cursory glance an hour later, to remind me that she needed to be taken for her walk! I called her over, and dangled a piece of cheese in front of her nose.

She licked her lips, and the cheese, but made no attempt to grab it and chew it! So I opened her mouth manually, dropped the cheese in, and closed her mouth! She chewed it happily, giving me sidelong glances to see if her prevarication in accepting it had any long term disastrous consequences! Stretching languorously after the slice of cheese, Lizzy waited expectantly for her ragi and milk breakfast, which she knew was the prelude to her walk. She kept darting glances to see when she would be called for it, because left on her own, she never did justice to the meal, leaving it more than three-quarters untouched.

"Lizzy . . . ." I beckoned to her.

She got up reluctantly, stretched half-heartedly, as if she knew she would be interrupted, then stood her ground, wondering at my next move.

"Lizzy!" I barked, impatiently. "Hurry up and come here," I said, gesturing to her plate.

Lizzy took baby steps towards her meal bowl, her head bowed, and her eyes still hooded, looking at me only from the corner of her eyes. She slouched low as she neared her bowl, refusing to get close to it.

By this time, my impatience knew no bounds, as I gave hurried glances at the racing clock. I caught hold of Lizzy firmly, lifted her bodily to her bowl, and quickly lumped her breakfast into her mouth, as she tried her level best to spit, slide or gag out the food as fast as I was trying to put it in!

"Lizzy! Just hurry up and eat it already! I don't have all day to cater to your needs!"

Lizzy merely slouched further into my arms, as she tried to make herself as invisible as possible! No amount of coaxing or cajoling or bribes work with her. I even showed her the b'day cake I had got for her, promising to give her a large size if she ate her breakfast fast!

"When did you get the cake?" akhilesh asked, astonished to find cake so early in the morning. "You baked it, huh?" he continued, incredulously.

"Of course not! Where would I be able to turn out such a wonderful concoction, son?"

"Its for us also?" he asked, lifting the lid of the cake box and peering into its contents intently, and liking the appearance and the smell, apparently.

"Not really. Lets see how much her majesty devours, and you guys might get some leftovers!" I replied, with a sly grin.

"We don't even have a dog's life!" bemoaned abhishek, dramatically, as he sat on the dining table, sipping his morning milk.

"Enough with all the negativity! Did you at least wish Lizzy on her b'day?" I rebuked them.

"Wish a dog!" abhishek asked derisively. "What will she understand even if I do "wish her"!

"Its just the warmth of your wishes, not the wishes per se. Why do you talk to her at times, when you know she doesn't understand? It's the same way. It's the warmth of your voice, not the words!"

With that, I took Lizzy for her walk, following her favorite route, where she was certain to come across a few rats to chase down, some squirrels on a tree to threaten, an odd cat on a building wall that she can try to grab, a barking dog marking its territory, and a couple of nice doggy friends on the way, who she can whisper sweet nothings to. These were not common on all the routes I took her out on. So we followed the one that she liked the most.

Sure enough, a white cat darted across the road on getting Lizzy's scent, raced up a wall, onto the roof of the garage, disappeared into a balcony! Lizzy saw it all in a fraction of a second! Unfortunately I saw it a second too late!

All I felt was a terrible jerk on my right shoulder and a streak of brown bolting out of my hands! I quickly steadied my tottering self.

"Lizzy!" I screamed, horrified at the route Lizzy was contemplating, in hot pursuit of the cat! I had a sense of déjà vu!

"Woof! Woof!" were the agonized high-pitched barks she gave standing below the wall and gazing up in desperation, to catch a glimpse of the cat! There was a long whine followed by a few more tormented barks. She jumped up the vertical wall, only to come slithering down, unable to get a grip, and not being nimble-footed enough like her arch nemesis, the cat! Lizzy was tormented that she could not scale the high wall and grasp the cat in her paws!

Some of the shopkeepers, in the midst of opening their shop and displaying their wares, stopped all work to stare awe-struck at this daft dog, which was trying her level best to do an Edmund Hillary on the wall! The cat for her part, was nowhere to be seen! But Lizzy, apparently, still managed to get her scent because she still continued frantically trying to scale the wall and jumping up for all her worth!

"Lizzy, that is quite enough! You have created enough of a scene early in the morning!" I remonstrated her sharply.

Lizzy whined plaintively in reply. I dragged her away from the scene. Quite a few onlookers had collected by now, to watch a crazy dog chase a cat! I almost expected a standing ovation for Lizzy's attempts to get at the cat!

"Ok, Lizzy girl, lets now enjoy the walk. You have started off with quite a lot of excitement for today. See there, that's Bruno," I said softly to her.

Bruno was this gorgeous golden retriever, a strapping male of 5 yrs. plus. He was an over-friendly dog brought on his walks by his male handler. His owners were obviously dog lovers because I had seen him in his house balcony, always free to roam around, no leash, and always happily wagging his tail at all the passer-byes. He was so happy to just be alive and his effervescent tail bore ample testimony to that!

Lizzy and he were obviously one of a kind. He was always overjoyed to meet Lizzy, who, after the initial introductions, would try to dominate him! Bruno never protested! He would acquiesce to every trauma Lizzy put him through, just happy to be around another dog! He was, of course, not amorous like Scotty! Just plain friendly and warm.

After a few minutes, Lizzy would get bored and growl at him or snap at him! Bruno, even then, didn't want to leave her! He was such a good-natured dog that he was willing to take whatever curveball Lizzy threw at him!

Goofy was another one of the regulars Lizzy met on this route. Yeah, the name made me grin always! He was another elegant and dapper cocker spaniel, a rich chocolate brown in color, with such big gentle eyes, that kept weeping from the sides all the time, that he looked like he had just jumped from out of a tragic movie! As a result of this, he had a permanent stain on the sides of either eye, the nasal side, with matted fur. He was a tad apprehensive of Lizzy, being the shorter of the two. Lizzy pretended to be unaware of his insecurities, boisterously jumping over him and trying to dominate him! Goofy always tugged helter-skelter at his leash, tried to get behind his walker's legs, but the moment Lizzy moved away from him, he decided that she was delectable when she wasn't anywhere close to him and he would sneak up behind her, sniffing curiously! Lizzy would jump up startled, and then give him the third degree! Poor Goofy, no way he could win with Lizzy! Her majesty did not tolerate being investigated in such an unceremonious manner!

In spite of all the happy doggy meetings by the roadside, Lizzy would still come running to me to continue the walk, without a care about romping with the other dogs. She would obediently stand while I slung the leash back on her and would trot along gaily, sniffing the ground for any fresh smells!

It was on one of these long walks that we stuck up a life-long friendship with Scotty and his owners.

Scotty, the completely-besotted-with-Lizzy Labrador, would lumber up into a trot on seeing his beloved Lizzy! His owner had a tough time controlling his energetic tugs on the leash! Lizzy had a funny way of getting around pulling her leash and making a dash for it . . . . she would yank the leash and then turn right around to face me! If I showed any laxity, she would wriggle right out of the body harness and escape to freedom! Initially we presumed it was because she was a pup and had not yet grown into her collar. But as she continued doing it, we realized she had developed this amazing technique of contorting her body into a fetal posture and in one swift jerk, take her head out of the collar, following which her front paws slid out and she was free! It turned out that the half an inch gap in the body harness, that was given out of consideration to her, so as to not make it overly tight, was enough to give her room space to maneuver out!

We wizened up after that!

The moment I realized she was up to her tricks, I would slide my hand down close to the collar so that she did not get wriggle space at all!

Lizzy did not struggle after that. She would try the trick but if she was out-maneuvered, she kept still, till I let her go. Of course, she knew us enough to realize that we would let her go and greet her compatriots each time, unless it was one of the strays.

Scotty wagged his luxurious tail endlessly, his tongue lolling happily along the side of his ample jaw, gazing moony eyed at Lizzy.

"Woof! Woof, woof woof . . . ." Lizzy yelled at him. "Stop mooning and play!" she seemed to say. She went up to Scotty's face and nipped his upper lip.

"Ouch! That hurt!" Scotty yelped. He then chased Lizzy down the road and for the next 10 minutes, they barked and chased and nipped each other playfully. Lizzy pounced on Scotty every 3 seconds to establish the exact hierarchy, and dropped him to the ground. Scotty always acquiesced and waited for Lizzy to get off his back in order to resume his devotion to her.

There was a sudden movement in the bushes and Lizzy lost all interest in Scotty! She raced across the road and dived into the shrubs to catch the rat, hotly pursued by Scotty!

"Lizzy! No! Dirty!" I yelled. Lizzy gave a disdainful look across to me and resumed her task of chasing the offending entity! Sometimes, Lizzy didn't take me seriously, only the task at hand.

"Scotty! Come back!" this by his agonized owner, who by now, had given up hopes of ever seeing a nice and clean dog he had brought along!

"Lizzy! That is dirty! Get back here right now!" I said in a stern voice.

Lizzy sat back on her haunches and gave me a dirty look! "woof!" "Woof! Woof!"

"Nothing doing! Come back here!"

She slowly trudged back. Scotty ran back to her joyfully, glad to get her attention again.

Soon Lizzy forgot all about the offending intruder, as she resumed her growling and nipping and pouncing of Scotty!

"Scotty forgets all about home and us when he is with Lizzy," remarked his owner, wryly. "You know, if we mention the name 'Lizzy' while he is eating or sleeping at home, he just drops whatever he is doing and rushes to investigate if Lizzy has really come!"

"Don't you get Scotty to play with other dogs on your street in your new locality?" I asked.

"Nobody else is so open and friendly. Everybody collects their precious dog to themselves and refuses to allow any mingling," he replied, sadly. "People are so narrow-minded and unfriendly. They should at least allow animals to get along."

Soon after that, we had to go our separate ways, since everybody was on work schedule.

"Lizzy, lets see who else we meet up on the way. Since its your b'day, we will go for a longer walk and see if we can get some more of your friends to greet you!" I remarked.

Lizzy was game to do anything which entailed a walk with her mistress! All those lovely smells, furry things to chase, even more furry germ-balls on four legs to play and bully over . . . . what more could a doggie want!

"Woof . . . . woof . . . . woof! Carry on!" she seemed to say, tongue hanging out in a lop-sided grin on the cute face.

A little while later, Jackie, a chocolate brown cocker spaniel came trudging along, held on a leash by his friendly dog-handler. He was a tad scared of Lizzy's over enthusiastic jumping and decided safety was of primary concern when Lizzy was around! So Jackie sniffed and retreated, sniffed and retreated! Lizzy looked at him quizzically, twisting her neck both ways to check out this new method of greeting.

"Hey . . . . get on with it! You check me out and then I check you out, and back and forth again. That's how its played. Here, let me show you," barked Lizzy, giving him a thorough hug, as she towered over him.

Jackie yelped in distress, his thin frame unable to bear Lizzy's bear hug! He retreated into the safety of his handler. Lizzy really got down to business!

"Hey . . . . c'mon . . . . you've got to play!" she woofed at him, hunching her fore legs with her rump in the air, the classic 'play' position.

"Woof! Woof!"

She darted at him from behind and then from the front, but Jackie would not be enticed! He did not like rough play! Lizzy soon lost interest in him as she discovered something smelling nice on the footpath. She pored over it in great concentration, racking her brain to fathom which animal the dung belonged to! Jackie came out from his safe dugout and sniffed Lizzy's behind with great loyalty! Lizzy jumped out of her skin at this intrusion, when her entire brain was doing justice to the 'treat' in front of her. She did not like disturbances from behind, especially from a chip of a dog who had the audacity to sneak up on her unawares!

"Gr . . . . woof!" Lizzy bared her teeth showing her displeasure.

"Lizzy! Stop it! You are scaring the poor dog! You are unfit to play!" I rebuked her, seeing Jackie scrounge up behind his handler's legs.

"What did I do? He wouldn't play and then he acted gross!" Lizzy barked back at me.

And so we left, Lizzy showing her great outrage at me and Jackie by chewing her leash and pulling it in the opposite direction!

Time was running out and I was about to call the walk to its end, when we met this trio of the most gorgeous golden retrievers, all belonging to one family! There were 2 adult dogs and one which looked to be a puppy still! As expected, Lizzy and I couldn't control our excitement and I followed Lizzy's lead to meet the trio. The owners did not look too happy at our proximity, so I called out that Lizzy is a friendly dog. I don't think I quite managed to convince the lady, but the man next to her, holding 2 of the leashes gave a half-hearted smile.

So while Lizzy and the dogs were busy getting to know each other, I stuck up a conversation with the owners. They apparently lived in an apartment not far from our complex. They had been living there for many many years.

Recently their dog had given a litter and they had decided to keep one for themselves, in spite of having 2 others. So I asked the obvious question, whether there was any voice of protest from the other members in their apartment block. The man smiled and replied in the negative and attributed it to the fact that they had stayed there for much longer than most of the other inhabitants in the complex.

Meanwhile, Lizzy had lost interest in the adults and was cornering the pup which was alternately cowering and glowering at Lizzy! Lizzy, for once, was at a loss for words. She did not understand this creature, which smelt like a dog, but did not do all the doggy things, like sniff or bark or whine or sit on its haunches as an invitation to play! She decided to investigate one level further.

"Woof!" she howled into the pups' ears! "C'mon. Get on with it. Decide you want to act like a dog or like a human, already!" Lizzy snorted.

"Eeow . . . . eeow eeow . . . . eeow . . . . !" yelped the poor pup and ran around its owners legs, winding the leash tightly around the man's legs!

"WOOF! WOOF!" yelled the adult dogs, crossly.

"Lets go" the lady called out agitatedly, running to catch up with the fleeing pup on its leash.

"I am so sorry," I apologized to the kind owner. "Lizzy is a little hyper-excitable and especially around pups, she kind of goes crazy," I explained.

He smiled. "Boxers are bouncy dogs, I know."

"Bad dog Lizzy. Can't behave like a lady, huh," I scolded Lizzy gently, not wanting to dampen her spirits on her b'day.

Lizzy, blissfully unaware of the commotion she had started, happily skipped along the way, none the worse for the whole mishap. She put the dogs out of her mind, the moment they left and looked around to see if there were any other dogs to catch up and share the day's wonders!

"Ok, young lady. We will head home now. I don't think you are going to meet any more of your buddies today," I remarked, and we made our way slowly home. Lizzy, apparently, had also had quite a measure of excitement for one day because she retreated back home quietly enough!

We played ball for a while in the courtyard. She was not too tired to 'fetch' ball even after such a long walk and so much howling! As usual, when she saw the large piece of grass near the drive, she went totally batty and dashed over it helter-skelter as was her wont! And then bounded up the flight of stairs, 3 at a time, to reach the front door of our house, waiting impatiently for me to open the door!

I left for work receiving many forlorn glances from Lizzy, which tore into my heart. Yeah, I guess I was getting unnecessarily emotional, since Lizzy did not understand the concept of birthdays at all. But I, the human did, and I felt bad to leave her alone, on this special day of hers, with just the maid.

On an impulse, I called up Scotty's owners and requested them to come down in the evening to give Lizzy some company.

On my way back from hospital, I managed to buy one plate of grilled chicken, with the masala washed off thoroughly, which I knew would thrill Lizzy no end! After all, what's a special day for dogs without non-vegetarian food! Also some special doggy biscuits and cookies!

I was, as a matter of fact, really charged up and excited . . . . I don't know about Lizzy!

I reached home with all my goodies and Lizzy would not let go of me, the moment I entered the door! Akhilesh helped me put all the packages on the center table, high away from Lizzy's nosy face!

"You seriously are going to have a party? For a dog?" my sons chorused incredulously!

"Yeah. What's wrong?" I replied nonchalantly.

"Nothing wrong ma. We knew you were going to be up to something weird!" they grinned. "Ok. We are off to play shuttle. Ma, hopefully you are not going to leave us out and keep all the dogs inside and party!"

"No dogs, only dog, as in only Scotty. Like I told you, lets kept this in-house. I don't think anybody would be magnanimous enough to tolerate a *bunch* of furry critters!"

"Lizzy down!" I screamed, as I saw my precious booty for the party toppling over as Lizzy tried to pry it open. "You scam artist! Wait till I get my hands on your butt!"

Lizzy skunked underneath the dining table, looking up at me with innocent eyes, sniffing the air to see if I was really riled or just faking it!

I stood near the edge of the table, threateningly. This was a game I played with her, pretending to be really angry, to see what her reaction would be. Lizzy crouched silently under the table, continuously sniffing the air. After a few minutes, she crept a little closer. I stood still. I expected her to close up on me soon, and she did . . . . slowly, cautiously. She came up to my dangling hand and gave it a light lick. I loved this moment when Lizzy was so suppliant and not an explosive bundle of energy! I savored these few seconds. Lizzy ventured a little further, wondering if she should expect a yell from me anytime. I retreated a few steps. Lizzy followed. Then gently, ever so silently, she placed her front paws on my chest and looked up into my face, lovingly. That beautiful boxer face with its tongue out and the kindest, most adoring eyes melting your heart, what more could any dog lover ask for.

I cupped her face lovingly in my hands and cooed sweet nothings to her. Lizzy, the little devil, lapped up all my love . . . . and then dashed to the food table again!

"Woof! Now that all is forgiven, you hand me over some of these lovely smelling treats," she seemed to say. Ever the opportunist!

"Lizzy, you get down right now. That's for later, when everybody is around!" I said sternly.

"Woof! Please please! Woof!"

"All right. Just one piece, since it is after all your b'day and you have had no treats since morning," I relented, approaching the table. Lizzy jumped around in joy, showing her delight by woofing a few more times!

I gave her a cookie.

Lizzy does not eat from your hands right away. Its painful giving her anything to eat! She needs to sniff it from different angles, give it the 'look' a few times, wait for it to make a threatening move . . . . after all of which, she will come a little closer and lick it tentatively, looking up at me every now and then to check what is the meter reading of my patience! Finally, she will relent and take the treat!

It was always better to just drop the food piece in question, before her majesty, hoping that it will be eaten before the ants get to it! She could do all this and get away with it, only because she was a single dog in this house. If she had had a companion, she wouldn't have got anything to eat!

I did not want to drop the cookie in case it leaves crumbs on the floor and we are invaded by ants! So I held on for a few minutes.

"C'mon Lizzy. Take the piece already!"

Lizzy continued sniffing delicately, interspersed with glances at me from the corner of her eyes.

"Lizzy!"

She licked the cookie, looked up at me. "Ok, chill. I like it. I'll take it," she seemed to say.

She took the cookie gracefully out of my hands and chewed on it contently, one eye on me in case I take it out of her mouth or yell at her to drop it!

The things I suffer in patience with this dog!

"Ok Lizzy. Now you behave. I need to get things organized so that you and Scotty can eat and enjoy without having to brawl for your food," I said, gesturing her to go away.

Lizzy stayed put. All the smells were too enticing for her to stay away!

I pushed her in front of me, as I went into another room to search for a second bowl for Scotty. I did not trust leaving Lizzy there in the living room with all the goodies!

Lizzy slunk her stump of a tail down and reluctantly left the living room.

I found a steel bowl, a left over from a previous dog perhaps, I thought. It was not very big but I reckoned it would suffice for just Scotty. I placed it in the living room diametrically opposite to Lizzy's bowl. For all her fastidiousness for food, Lizzy did take kindly to another dog partaking what she considered her home's properties! She will go tooth and nail for it, and I did not want fur flying in the midst of a party! Especially when the subject in question was non-vegetarian food, I was quite sure Scotty will give as good as he gets!

I placed a water bowl next to the food bowl just in case he felt thirsty after panting behind Lizzy! There was every chance that Scotty would adoringly look at Lizzy and nothing beyond that! But I liked to cover all the options.

I arranged the table with the cake in the center. The chicken plate was well protected by all the other food items around it, so that Lizzy did not make a dash for it when we were not looking! Lizzy would not move away from the table and kept her eyes locked on it.

Scotty, when he came, just bolted out of the lift, as boisterous as ever! He headed straight for Lizzy! We were all blurry shapes to him, about which he couldn't care less! His owners were panting to keep him under a tight leash, and failing miserably! He was a hefty Labrador!

Lizzy stood up, and not in a very friendly manner. Normally she would race across the hall to meet him mid-way and their meeting would be catastrophic for the furniture around! But today, she stood her ground. Before he could reach Lizzy, Scotty's nostrils were bombarded by all these amazing smells from the dining table! He stopped suddenly, sniffed the air . . . . and made a U-turn towards the dining table! Lizzy preceded him and stood guard, baring her teeth soundlessly!

Before the fur could fly, I dragged both of them out into the balcony! And shut the door firmly! I could hear Lizzy's growls and Scotty, finding Lizzy all to himself, and not side-tracked by enticing smells, went back to his usual adoring self, adoring Lizzy ie! But Lizzy did not like being locked up, away from people. She was so totally a people dog! She would rather be denied the food but could not be away from people! So she kept up a regular barking session!

I took the time to greet my guests.

Everybody felt that it was better to get the dogs eating and then settle down to talk amongst ourselves.

I got the candle going on the cake. We let the dogs in with stern warnings to both to 'behave'! With tongues lolling, and eyes fixed on the food on the table, both sat on their haunches waiting expectantly. I cut the cake by lifting Lizzy up on to the table, which she acquiesced quite embarrassedly. I gave them both a piece of it in their bowls. Lizzy licked it and licked it for all she was worth. Finally, as the piece was getting licked off the bowl, she managed to take it into her mouth. Her bowl was spotlessly clean after that! Scotty was making heavy weather of it! He decided he did not like the sweet pineapple taste after all!

I threw a few cookies into the air and both dogs jumped up to grab it. Lizzy, being lighter, managed to jump faster and higher and got the cookies both times. Scotty's owners entered the fray and for a while there was general bedlam, as everybody was throwing cookies and dog biscuits into the air and the dogs were jumping helter-skelter, interspersed with Lizzy's growls and Scotty's yelps as Lizzy sometimes grabbed a handful of his mouth in trying to get to the cookie first! She was competitive!

It was at this point that my two tired sons entered the house and apparently, they could hear the cacophony 3 floors down, as they got into the elevator! They rang the bell cautiously at first, and then furiously 2-3 times as there was no response to the first ring! Obviously, all the living beings inside were busy chasing biscuits and cookies, humans included!

Surveying her world from the bay window . . . just a day in
Lizzy's comfortable life!

Watchful when i approach her. She's always in fear that i feed her!

The sofa is her comfort zone. The morning siesta!

Happy to play. Sitting in anticipation.

Snack time! Lizzy with her chew stick in her corner.

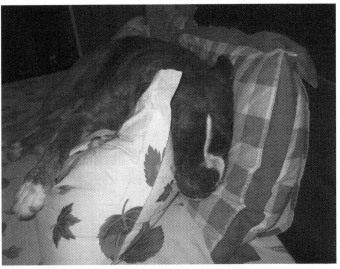

Cosy snooze on a winter's morning. One of Lizzy's favorite positions!

Warm comfort on the thick quilt on a cold day. This is how she spends her mornings when i am out.

I got this just as she was making her self comfortable on my bed! That's her looking enquiringly at me! Whatcha doing here? Come to disturb me?

I could write a book on just how many poses she sleeps in on my bed! This is another one of her sleeping joys on cold days.

After a while, during which my sons had reached boiling point, Lizzy and Scotty both set up loud barks and raced towards the door! I pushed them aside and opened the door. Both dogs jumped in great enjoyment on the 2 unsuspecting humans standing bemused outside! I ushered them in and shushed the dogs.

"Ok. Now for the main course!" I announced grandly. "Who wants chicken? Slurpy slurpy chicken anyone!" I called out enticingly.

"Woof!"

"Woof!" from Scotty.

"Ok you guys, I am going to put equal pieces of chicken in either bowl and you will both behave and eat only out of your respective bowls!" I warned.

"Yeah ma. You could also try teaching them some table manners, while you are at it!" Abhishek said slyly.

I glared at him and proceeded to divide the chicken pieces into their bowls. Then I took their bowls and shifted the dogs along with their goodies onto the balcony.

I stood guard there for awhile. Then I went into the living room to keep the humans in conversation.

There was peace for the next 3 minutes exactly. Then I heard a low growl. A deep-throated warning to stay off!

I stopped my conversation mid-way and hurriedly walked outside to maintain peace.

I was just in time to see Lizzy's bared teeth making faces at Scotty. Scotty had polished off his meal and was cozying up to Lizzy to see if his beloved would spare a few ribs for him! But Lizzy was way too possessive about non-vegetarian food and gave him ample indication that she would defend her meal till her last breath! It was a face-off!

Lizzy's low-throated rumbles sounded like distant thunder! But that did not seem to be deterring Scotty! He pranced around Lizzy, his tail wagging nineteen to the dozen! Scotty could hold up on his own in a fight, if it were to come to that! He was ably built and unless he surrendered out of abject devotion to Lizzy, there was no way Lizzy was going to do him any damage!

I got in quietly between Lizzy and Scotty. Scotty looked up at me, "hey, what's with you playing spoil-sport here?" he seemed to ask.

Lizzy chomped down her chicken, keeping a watchful eye on the unfolding events. She was used to me around her meal, but did not like Scotty's eager-beaver attitude where meal times with her favorite menu was concerned.

"Scotty no", I said firmly. "Go back to your owners. You finished your meal."

Scotty pretended not to understand. He whined to see if that would get him some pieces from Lizzy's plate.

"Scotty come"! admonished his owner. "You are not allowed any non-vegetarian food, and now you want more!"

Scotty stood his ground. He looked uncertainly at Lizzy. Lizzy bared her teeth as a warning of worse to come. Scotty wagged his bushy tail and appeared to smile! Lizzy was not impressed! She got back to munching the bone with a wary eye on the crowd around her, human and animal!

"Scotty!" his owner called out again, sternly.

Scotty wagged his tail and trotted up to his owner. He stood at the door of the balcony and threw a longing glance at Lizzy. Lizzy did not bother to look up from her bowl! I followed Scotty out into the living room and continued the conversation.

"Ma, Lizzy is not eating. She is standing at the balcony door and waiting," my sons chorused.

"Lizzy, you are being so mean! If you didn't want the chicken, you could have given it to Scotty," I protested.

Lizzy wagged her short tail, or her entire rump! She opened her mouth in a half pant and put her tongue out to lick me endearingly.

So I joined her in the balcony while she chomped through the rest of her food. Scotty galloped to the balcony and stood at the door, wagging his tail and grinning at Lizzy. Lizzy finished her chicken and then looked around to see if there were any more pieces waiting to be devoured. She sniffed Scotty's bowl, and finding no vestige of past food there, decided it was time to play!

So she bounded up to Scotty and soon there was pandemonium there, as they chased each other! As is her wont, Lizzy loves taking flying leaps over all obstruction, instead of circumventing it! So she flew over the living room settee, over the peg tables, and then onto the bed! Scotty, not to be outdone, tried leaping over the settee . . . . and realized too late, that his ample girth would not allow him to fly over objects! So he suffered an ungainly crash into the settee and was none the worse for it! He shook himself, and set off in hot pursuit of his lady love in a jiffy! This time he made sure to go around the obstacles, instead of over them, which Lizzy managed to do with utmost ease.

He did manage to jump onto the bed to join Lizzy! The two of them ran in circles trying to catch each other and pin them down! I came running inside when I heard continuous growls and barks!

"Lizzy! The bed is not the place to play, especially with so much fur from Scotty flowing all over!" I yelled. "Get down right now!"

No sooner had the words left my mouth, Lizzy took a flying leap out of the bed. Scotty tried imitating her, and landed bang onto the peg table kept near the bed, breaking the glass top into a million pieces! There was glass scattered all over the bedroom floor.

I stood there, agape with horror! I could well imagine the reaction of my husband! Especially since the deed was done by a 4-legged fur ball . . . . a species not too fancied by my dear husband!

I choked back my despair and brushed off the profuse apologies of Scotty's owners. What was done, was done and could not be undone. I resolved never to allow another animal into the room. Lesson learnt, I said to myself.

Lizzy crouched in a corner, behind the single settee, trying to be as unobtrusive as possible. She knew she was somehow linked to the huge noise that had just shattered the peace and which caused her mistress to totally stop talking . . . . which was very unusual as far as Lizzy was concerned, and which did not bode well for anybody's welfare!

Scotty, for his part, found everything hugely amusing! He kept eyeing Lizzy behind the settee, and wagged his tail even harder, thinking all this was another game! He barked loudly for good measure to drag Lizzy's attention to him. But Lizzy glanced at him cursorily and focused all her attention on me, feeling guilty as hell!

I saw the forlorn look on her cute little face, and I decided, nothing was worth spoiling Lizzy's first b'day!

So I called out to her. "Lizzy! Come here baby. Its ok," I smiled at her.

Lizzy came out of her secure place, warming up to my easy tone.

"Lizzy, what did you do?" my son sneakily called out.

Lizzy stopped dead in her tracks. She looked up at Abhishek and then at me, confused.

"Lizzy . . . . what did you do? You did something bad," my sons chorused, hugely enjoying the guilt on Lizzy's face and her discomfiture.

Lizzy's tail was right down and her eyes refused to meet mine. She shrunk to as small an object as she could and tried to slink away. Having come out of a protective barricade and finding none as she sauntered to meet me, Lizzy was really apprehensive.

"No, no Lizzy. Don't listen to the dirty boys. Come here baby," I crooned.

Lizzy gave me a dizzy look. "Look here you guys, am I getting punished or not? Decide so that I know what to do," she seemed to say.

"Boys, keep quiet! Its her b'day! You should not make her feel so bad. Cut it out!"

They relented. "Sorry Lizzy, sorry Lizzy. Come here baby girl," they cajoled.

'Sorry' was a word that somehow triggered Lizzy to go berserk! I am sure she didn't understand the word per se. But she always acted as if the floodgates of her emotions had been opened! She jumped up at them and proceeded to lick their faces thoroughly!

"Lizzy stop! Lizzy!" they screeched. Once Lizzy starts her vigorous welcome licks, there's no holding her back! She makes sure she gets every centimeter of the face! It is pretty disgusting to be covered in dog drool all over your face, especially since the boys had just had their baths after an energetic game of badminton.

Lizzy was in full flow. Scotty joined in, thinking it was some new game. He caught hold of Lizzy's rear legs in his mouth and proceeded to yank it. Lizzy dropped off the boys and turned around to attack Scotty. Soon they were all rolling around on the living room floor, humans and animals!

"You go Scotty! Get Lizzy!" the boys shouted, scowling at the mess Lizzy had made of their faces.

Lizzy was violently defending her honor against Scotty and winning by the looks of it. They were chasing each other helter-skelter and Scotty's owners never knew what hit them, when the 2 dogs came onto their settee at full speed! They were so intent on watching some programme on TV that they had not anticipated their free fall!

"Scotty!" they screeched in unison.

Scotty and Lizzy were deaf to everything but their yelps and growls.

I laughed, enjoying the mirth all around. "Let them enjoy their day today. They hardly get to meet nowadays," I said.

"I know. And Scotty doesn't get anyone to play rough stuff like this," they sighed.

"Well, here we all play rough with Lizzy! Especially on the bed and Lizzy is used to this kind of boisterous play-fighting all the time."

Sensing that all the humans attention was on her, Lizzy was in full force. She barked, growled, nipped and scratched Scotty. But in all this, both of them were extremely careful not to draw blood. As soon as I decided to step aside and clear the table, Lizzy lost interest in Scotty! She wanted my attention on her all the time!

"Boys, keep calling out to Lizzy so that she plays with Scotty for some more time. Show them the balloons and bounce them around the dogs. I will clear the mess," I called out to the boys.

"Lizzy! Choo Scotty, choo Scotty! C'mon, lets see what else you got," Abhishek exclaimed.

Lizzy decided her humans needed protection from the rogue dog Scotty! So she barked loudly to announce her intention and chased Scotty, head lowered as if she intended to head butt him! Scotty, bulky as he was, realized rather too slowly that Lizzy was coming at him! By the time he got up on all fours to defend himself, Lizzy had launched herself at him! He went flying, legs flaying in the air, and a ton of fur forming a halo around him! Lizzy jumped him and sat down on him, looking down onto his face with low growls!

Even from that position, Scotty looked up adoringly at Lizzy, thumping his tail on the floor, in total acquiescence.

"Scotty! Get up and show some manhood, you love struck fur ball!" his owners yelled derisively, laughing at the totally besotted Scotty.

Scotty turned around at them, gave a small grin and looked up again at Lizzy, like the sun was shining out of her head.

"Scotty you are such a numbskull! Get up!"

Scotty decided he had to defend himself after all. He tried getting up, but Lizzy wouldn't get off him! He lay back and tried licking Lizzy's face.

"Scotty! You disgusting so-and-so!"

"Woof!" and suddenly Scotty got up with a heave. Lizzy was thrown down before she could say 'hallelujah'! But she managed to collect herself, turned around and jumped Scotty again. This time, Scotty was prepared.

He met her head on and they started all over again, with constant encouragements from my sons.

I took this opportunity to clear the glass pieces in the room and sweep all the minute pieces away. Most of the b'day dishes were over, barring a few doggie cookies. I brought them out to the living room to be given to the dogs after their showdown!

By the time I finished clearing the mess of fur and bits and pieces of food in the living room, the dogs called a truce. Both were panting and could not even drink the water in the bowls for want of oxygen!

They sat down next to their water bowls, looking comically up at me! "Hey boys, give them some ice-cold water to drink. See if they like it," I said.

Scotty lapped it up. Lizzy had a few sips, and then decided it was too weird to continue and anyway, it did not quench her thirst. So she retreated back and sat on her haunches, waiting for normal water. Scotty hung around to drink nearly half a bottle! Labradors, they say, eat anything, and that was so true with Scotty. He washed it down with 2 or 3 cookies and then sat down panting, a very satisfied look on his face. He looked around once or twice to see if his beloved Lizzy was still around and then gave a huge sigh of satisfaction. All was well in Scotty's world!

Lizzy took the cookies too! She looked at the cold water like it was some kind of Chinese torture and backed off as soon as the boys got the bowl close to her mouth!

She retreated next to my feet as I reclined on the settee. Scotty followed her every move and seeing her settled, decided that he did not have the strength to move close to her and so he put his nose on his front paws and went to sleep!

"Scotty, come lets go home," his owners called out.

Scotty twitched his ears and continued sleeping!

"Scotty!" shouted his astounded owners. "You like Lizzy more than us now, is it? Ok you stay here and we will go."

Scotty did not move, but he deigned to open his eyes and look up at them, without moving his head! "Ok, what's the fuss about. Cant you see we are all peaceful in here? Let me get some shut-eye, if you don't mind," his eyes said, proclaiming his annoyance!

"Fine, we will leave him here," saying that they proceeded towards the door.

Scotty jerked his head up, looked at Lizzy, still reclining peacefully next to my feet, unflinching. He was quite undecided as to his next course of action. He stared back at his owners, decided they meant business, and lopped across to them. He stood next to the door and looked back at Lizzy.

Lizzy got up too as I stood up to bid farewell to the guests. She grudgingly walked across to the door, gave Scotty a nuzzle and then stood near the door, waiting.

"I am not going out anywhere Lizzy, they are. You want to go with them?" I asked gently.

"Call Lizzy in otherwise she may run off and away," Scotty's owners cautioned.

"Don't worry about Lizzy. She will not go anywhere without me, even if the door is opened and even if you call her to go with you," I remarked smilingly.

"Really, shall I call her then?"

"Try it. She won't leave me and go."

So they tried their level best to entice her, showing her Scotty first going away in the elevator, then offering a cookie and calling out to her, but Lizzy, the faithful baby

119

she was, would not be tempted at all. She kept giving backward glances to see if I would accompany her in the journey, but finding me standing still next to the door, Lizzy retreated back to me. Ever the faithful she was.

# (12)

## Holiday plans

**H**aving a pet meant not only feeding them and looking after them, but also giving them your time. What every pet wants is not an elaborate meal or a luxurious bed to sleep on, but just the undivided attention of their loved humans.

I already felt guilty about leaving Lizzy alone at home from 9 am to 3 pm, while I went out to work. I did not feel the maid compensated for my absence. So going out for any event after that was an ordeal for me, which my family would not understand.

Any outing scheduled for the evening or night, brought out vociferous protests from me. My sons reluctantly tried to understand where that was coming from, but my husband felt cheated and annoyed at my, what he considered, irrational behavior. There was nothing I could say or do, that convinced him otherwise. I really felt infinitely sad and sorry to leave Lizzy all alone, even for 2-3 hours. We had a pact, the boys and I, that we would try and take Lizzy with us, everywhere we could even if she had to be left in the car for some time, provided of course, it was not hot outside. Most times, I cajoled one of my sons to stay in the car with her, which brought forth a volley of protests, but they acquiesced! Of course, a half hour entrapment in the car in cooler climates was not something I was averse to.

It was when we had dinner plans that I really whined and tried my level best to get out of! After a while, my husband saw through all my 'headaches' and 'tired feeling' excuses for what they actually were . . . . a plea to stay back home to keep Lizzy company! I tried bargaining for a lunch out or a breakfast out, when my maid would stand in, but most times a Saturday night dinner and movie became imperative in our routine lives and we had to leave Lizzy alone at home.

When she was a baby, I tried putting her in the third bedroom and leaving the door open, with 2 sturdy dinner table chairs at the doorway, seat of one facing the other, one on top, to form a barricade, so that she does not wander out, but at the same time, does not feel cooped up inside. Lizzy, since she was always wiry and scrawny, when a pup, learnt the trick to climb onto the chairs and wriggle out through the spaces and break into freedom and then run havoc in the living room!

So that having failed, we resorted to keeping her in the living room, and closing all the other doors, with the balcony being left open. Lizzy played tug-of-war with all the furniture, which by the time we came back, looked like the middle-east crisis had hit our house!

There was another flop side to this side show. Lizzy would be so overjoyed to see us back, that she would have toilet 'mishaps' the moment she saw us! So we had to tiptoe into the apartment complex . . . . which obviously did not bode well for my husband's temperament! He did not like adjusting for non-humans! He especially felt insulted that he had to work around Lizzy's personality quirks!

Lizzy would bark the place down on hearing or smelling us arrive, and I would forever be apprehensive that the neighbors would object to the noise in the dead of the night! Then of course, she would promptly pee right behind the door in her anxiety to welcome us, and then flee to the farthest corner of the living room, when we opened the door, feeling very guilty. Torn between guilt and joy, Lizzy would bound helter-skelter on the sofas, causing endless agony to my husband! And there was the added irritation of trying to avoid all her 'mishaps' or 'landmines' as we called them!

So ultimately, we would greet Lizzy for a few seconds and proceed to clean up the mess in the house before taking a breath of relief! One of the boys would be in-charge of taking Lizzy down after our initial greeting, so that she could completely empty her bladder and continue her joyous greeting of us! I would hear endless mutterings from the son who had to help me clean the 'landmines' inside the house! Lizzy would look very doubtfully at all the dark looks and toned down curses from both of us after she returned from her trip downstairs, sniffing the air expectantly, to know if she were still in the doghouse or all was well!

In all of this, my husband would close the bedroom door and curl up to go to sleep, determined not to get involved in 'petty' stuff! He also hated the fact that his house was one big bathroom! He figured, since we desired the dog, we get the privilege to clean up afterward! Lizzy, for her part, sensed the disdain he had for her, and did not venture to shower her affection on him on our return. His disgust stemmed from the fact that things were not normal with his family with the advent of a four-legged mutt!

So finally, we resigned ourselves to leaving her out in the balcony. Of course, this happened only later after she grew big enough such that she could not slip through the grills of the balcony and fall 3 floors down! But by this time, my sofa set, the dining table chairs and cushion, the lower hanging shelves, all had taken a merry beating at her paws and jaws!

We also had to make sure that none of the chewable or breakable items were remaining in the balcony while we were gone. Lizzy vent her anger on any of such objects, which would be in total tatters by the time we came back, which was what happened to the brooms and mops that we had forgotten were kept behind the balcony door and which we found chewed into pieces and strewn all over the balcony, covered with Lizzy's pee liberally, once on coming back from a late night movie!

Yeah, we got the message loud and clear . . . . Lizzy did not like being alone and made her disapproval very obvious.

We wizened up as the months went by and slowly made the area less disaster prone. We would empty her bladder 3 or 4 times, before leaving. We would also give her very little water prior to such a plan. We had to clear the balcony of all and every item. Thankfully the balcony grills were made out of metal! We left a few of her favorite chew toys with her on the balcony, so that she could amuse herself while we were away.

Fortunately, Lizzy was not the barking sort and although the security guard has told us that the moment we left, Lizzy would bark for a while, she would keep it down after a few cursory protests! So we didn't get any flak from the neighbors!

Her toilet 'mishaps' did not stop! We would find one or two puddles at the far end of the balcony. Lizzy, like most animals, avoided her excrement in whatever form. So she made sure she voided in a remote corner, so that she had ample space to still curl up and snooze, without touching the offending body fluid. Yes, it was definitely easier to clean the balcony landmines since just pouring buckets of water would sweep it all down into the garden.

This was also an arrangement entirely acceptable to my husband and he did not curl up his nose in disgust now each time we returned home! Also, he proclaimed that the house did not smell like a garbage truck had unloaded its items inside, anymore!

If, on the other hand, we were taking Lizzy out with us on one of these jaunts, there would be a prelude to informing about the said outing to Lizzy, a little like foreplay!

"Lizzy, we are going 'tata'," I would sing slyly.

Lizzy's ears perked up and she looked up at me with a jerk of her head!

"Lizzy 'tata' bye bye," abhishek called out.

Lizzy got up and whimpered.

"You stay here," I said sternly, keeping a straight face, wiggling a finger at her, tauntingly.

Lizzy's whimpering got louder and she wailed in agony. "Woof, woof!"

"No. You stay here, we are going 'tata',"

"Woof, woof," from a now thoroughly agitated Lizzy. "You guys! I wanna come too," Lizzy whined plaintively.

"Lizzy stay here!"

Lizzy's cries reached herculean proportions! She howled like a wolf and ran to the front door, jumping in anticipation.

"Yeah right. Just because you are standing at the door, you think I am gonna take you? Lizzy stay here!"

Poor Lizzy, got very excited and started barking non-stop, eyes dilated, her whole body in a state of total agitation, thinking the worst! "Lizzy you stay here," we continued teasing her. I think Lizzy realized after a while that we were going out and that her acquiescence was required for her being taken out, hence the drama! So although she would charge out of the door before us, pre-empting our move, she still got very agitated at the mention of 'tata bye-bye'. It was more like, 'ok guys, I know you are going out and probably taking me too, but I am just howling the place down to make sure that you know that I don't want to be left behind!"

Once we started the tease, we would definitely take her.

Lizzy started jumping in front of the elevator, begging not to be left behind!

"Lizzy, hang on. Let me get your leash on properly," I beseeched, trying to steady a hopping, volatile boxer. She wouldn't turn her head for me to slip the harness around her neck.

"Lizzy!" abhishek ordered. "Sit still, otherwise we will really leave you behind!"

As if Lizzy understood a word of that! She looked up at him quizzically. "Woof!" and then she whimpered long, in protest.

Finally we got the harness around her and I handed the leash over to him. In this high strung state, I couldn't have held on to her as we proceeded towards the car! Lizzy pulls so hard that she overpowers even a well-abled person into imbalance! And me with my high heels, I would have been on the floor the moment the lift doors opened!

It took Abhishek all his strength in his two hands to get a grip on the charging Lizzy! I also had to keep a distance behind her otherwise, in her haste to follow me, she would drag the person holding her leash, with total disregard for safety!

Once near the car, her eagerness to enter the car knew no bounds! My car has suffered innumerable scratches in the process and I have still not got it re-painted! Of course, my husband's lack of detail helps in my not getting flak for it!

As soon as the car door opened, Lizzy jumped in like the devils were after her. Once inside, she chose a window and happily sat down on her haunches.

"C'mon you all. Get it. The evening is not getting any younger!" she seemed to say!

"Yeah right. I have to squeeze into the left over space, after her majesty's big bum is occupied," akhilesh snorted derisively.

In response, Lizzy moved, ever so slightly, to give his face a soft lick, just as he was letting himself in. "Aw, Lizzy! I just washed my face!" he scowled. Lizzy was just too pleased with life to take offence at this protest! She was going out with her three beloved humans! What more could a doggy heart want?!

There was always a foreboding in my heart when the day would come and we had to leave Lizzy for a long duration, like for a few days. I could entrust my maid for 2-3 days, but more than that I knew would become a problem.

Out of the blue, my husband decided that we would all go on a road trip to Kerala, God's own country, in South India, with his sister's family. I was torn between being overjoyed and apprehensive. Lizzy's food was going to be a big problem, especially if I was not around. In my absence, Lizzy refuses to eat or even drink water. She is a tad ok if the boys are around.

As I was mulling over this fact, my maid suggested that she would sleep over and look after Lizzy for those days. The food issue was also sorted out by arranging for meat or chicken to be brought in the mornings and bread with milk in the evenings. I was still uncertain about the whole thing because I was scared about Lizzy's fate at the end of our 5-day road trip. I did not trust my maid to be as devoted to a dog as we were, especially behind my back, although I had promised her ample remuneration for looking after Lizzy.

The next couple of days were a flurry of activity as I got down to organizing the daily routine for my maid with Lizzy. I had to get money out for 5 days of food and a little side snack for the maid as well. It was decided that the day we left early in the morning, my maid would finish her other job in another house, take Lizzy for a walk and then reach home to leave Lizzy, go to the market, get the meat, boil the meat and then wait for it to cool before feeding it to her. Then she would go to her house nearby, have her lunch and come back to clean up after Lizzy and stay with her for a while. She would then leave for her afternoon job and return in time to take Lizzy for her evening walk and meal. Subsequently, she would have her dinner at her house, and then stay put for the night with Lizzy. I could foresee a millions things going wrong with all this!

"Ma, its only for 5 days. It will do Lizzy good to be away from us for a while. She's a big dog now ma. She will cope," my elder son chirped.

"She's only 2 yrs. old and for a dog, they prefer being with their humans and do not want a honorary gap of separation!" I retorted. "Only humans want some time off from each other."

I looked at Lizzy. She was sleeping peacefully next to the settee, oblivious to the machivalean intentions of her beloved humans, whom she trusted implicitly. I felt a rush of emotion for her. I got up and sat down next to her on the ground, passed my hand gently through her fur. Lizzy tweaked her eyes and looked up from her dreamy state. She accepted my affection with a gentle show of her tongue and closed her eyes. I hugged her! I couldn't resist it! I put my arms around her and nuzzled the face and inhaled the lovely doggy smell. Lizzy had a sweet smell and not the dusky odor associated with most dogs. I always believed it was because of her pure vegetarian diet!

"If your mother hugged us and cuddled us half the number of times that she does for the dog, I think we would all be considered lucky," my husband remarked wryly, observing my ministrations.

"Oh no. Don't remind her papa. She will do it and I don't like it!" abhishek exclaimed.'

"Why what's wrong? Its just a hug," akhilesh countered, who loved being hugged and cuddled.

Lizzy basked in all the sudden attention. But as my hugs and kisses got tighter and more intense, she sat up. "Ok, what's up? What's with the sudden rush of emotion?" she looked quizzically at me, slightly suspicious by now.

I pulled her onto my lap and hugged her again. I felt so awful about leaving her for 5 whole days. She had never been left even for one day.

"Ma, if you start with your tears now, we will leave you behind with Lizzy!" my sons threatened.

I smiled. "That would be all right." I sneaked a glance at my husband and as expected he was looking at me quietly, his mouth turned down in scorn.

"So the dog is more important than us," he enquired chillingly.

"I knew that was coming!" I exclaimed. "See, I would behave the same way if any of you were left behind all alone. Don't you understand? Do you remember how tearful I always was when we had to leave one of the boys with my parents for months, during our army transfers?"

He didn't look very convinced. I let it go. Nobody understands the passion an animal lover has for the 4-legged species. This was an oft-repeated argument which I knew had no closure!

And so the day arrived. We escaped into the van with our luggage while Lizzy was out on her morning walk with the maid. The arrangement was that the maid would not come along the main roads where there was a chance that we would cross them and Lizzy would yank her leash on smelling me out. Lizzy didn't have a clue that when she left on the morning walk, rather jauntily, she would not get to see us for the next 5 days.

I was so tempted to call up the house telephone the whole morning to find out how Lizzy was coping. But I resisted the attempt and joined in among the bonhomie. The driver was very helpful, pointing all the important landmarks along the way. By lunch hour, I could not control it any longer. As we stopped to eat, I called up the house number. My maid did not pick up the first 2 times I called. I was getting a tad panicky! Abhishek came over, seeing a harassed look on my face.

"She's ok ma. Don't worry. She will just think we have all left for work and school as usual and only after 3 pm she will start missing us," he reassured.

The maid picked up on the 3rd ring and I was in tears when I enquired about Lizzy.

"She's fine madam," the maid assuaged me. "She did not finish her meal of chicken in the morning. She is now having a little more and I am sure she will finish it by evening. I will be here with her. I had taken her with me when I went out to work and tied her up there while I finished my work. She was no trouble. Tomorrow, I will leave her loose to chase all the crows and squirrels!"

"Don't leave her alone in the house for too long, especially in the evening and night."

The countryside was so beautifully green and rich and the company inside the car so animated, that I left Lizzy in the back of my mind for a while. I rang up again at 8 pm and all was well with Lizzy. She searched for us vigorously when she returned from her evening walk and not finding anyone, she curled up on the balcony sniffing plaintively. I asked her to put Lizzy on the phone.

"Lizzy . . . . Lizzy . . . ." I called out.

Silence from the other side.

"Lizzy . . . . hello sweetie-pie. What are you doing? Hi Lizzy . . . ." I cooed.

"She is not reacting much," my maid replied. "She is going away from the receiver."

"Ok. Let her go. She doesn't understand, I guess," I said sadly.

I continued to call up, on and off over the next 5 days, always trying to get Lizzy to bark or acknowledge my voice somehow. But Lizzy never responded. The maid claimed Lizzy was eating well and that whatever she left from the morning meal she tried to finish off by evening or night. So that was quite reassuring. Surprisingly, Lizzy did not create any mayhem while being left alone by the maid in the mornings and in the evening. I expected some sort of dismayed reaction from the maid each time I made a call home, saying that Lizzy had destroyed this or that! But that never came.

When we returned home late in the evening after 5 days, we tiptoed into the house so as to surprise Lizzy. The surprise was on us!

Lizzy had left for her evening walk with the maid and we came back to an empty house. I quickly organized things so as to not to leave any obstacles in Lizzy's path when she returned, for in her enthusiasm to greet us, I was sure she would topple and break every thing around!

Lizzy entered the front door and we went into hiding. She came over to her water bowl and then stopped suddenly, sniffing the air. She turned around to the master bedroom and sniffed. Not sure of whether the whiff of us was actually around or if it was just a figment of her imagination, she trotted up to the bedroom, stopped at the door and sniffed vigorously again. Her nose was assailed by the smell of our luggage and our clothes and the presence of us behind the door, so her small tail started wagging gently.

My maid standing behind, watching all the drama, started giggling. Lizzy turned back to look at her, then looked into the room and gave a short bark!

"Woof," she said. "Hey, I think you guys are there, but I can't see you and I now don't know what to do," she seemed to say.

I gave a low whistle from behind the door, the once familiar whistle Lizzy has grown up with, hearing from when she was a pup. Lizzy bounded into the room, looking in the other direction, over the bed where she expected us to be lying or sitting. This was too much for akhilesh! He stumbled out of the hiding place behind the door, clutching his stomach in laughter!

"Hey you dodo! You couldn't smell us hiding behind the door, huh!"

"Hi baby! How you doing my darling Lizzy!" I cooed.

Lizzy went berserk! She lunged at me trying to lick my face, then she jumped onto to my 2 sons and tried licking them! So for the next few minutes, there was a lot of yelling, hugging and kissing going on, interspersed with tender endearments! Lizzy was alternately barking in joy, yelping in pain as she got hugged a little too tightly by all of us and jumping from one human to another in her confusion to lick all of us! She was so happy to see us that her joy knew no bounds and she had no clue how to or whom to greet! She managed to lick all of us and leave us in disarray!

My husband chose to stay away from all this bonhomie! He did not approve of kisses and licks between animal and humans!

In between Lizzy's devoted licks and my unpacking, I managed to enquire from the maid about Lizzy's diet the previous 5 days and if there any untoward health concerns. Lizzy, apparently, had been a picture of good behavior but her eating left a lot to be decided! She had eaten only half her meals in the last 3 days, refusing to touch the meat or the milk in the evening and it all had to be thrown out! She would just greet my maid on her arrival and then proceed to curl up and sleep on the balcony.

"Lizzy," I chided her. "You have been a very bad girl, not eating your meals properly."

Lizzy did not understand the words but my tone made her tail go down and slink away in gloom!

"Oh c'mon Lizzy, your majesty! Such a drama queen!" chided abhishek.

Lizzy perked her ears up. Was everything well now? She looked up at him quizzically. Then she stole a glance at me.

I stared back at her unblinkingly. Time stood still as Lizzy and I locked eyes for a considerable period of time. Lizzy is such a fun-loving spirited girl that being steady and inactive like this is abhorrent to her! So slowly, quietly, she sniffed the air and took a few baby steps towards me. She didn't take her eyes off me all this time. I stood still wanting to play this out till its logical end!

Lizzy stood at my feet, looked up. Not finding any response, she quietly licked my hand. I smiled. That was enough! Lizzy leapt up and placed her paws on my chest, trying to get her tongue onto my face.

"Lizzu . . . . ," I cooed, and hugged her.

Lizzy danced in joy, her short stump of a tail wagging uncontrollably! She jumped up trying to lick my face, uttering short squeals of elation! Then she hopped madly around the living room, jumping over sofas and peg tables, ecstatic and finally able to express it unabashedly! She sat on the sofa and looked at us, her human family, in total devotion, ears flat and drooling love and delight! Then she took a flying leap at me, sure in the knowledge that I will hold and not let her fall! I held her fast, but boy, she was a hefty weight! I was used to Lizzy's madcap running around when she greeted us after a time out, so I was expecting her to do just that!

She followed me like a lamb all through the day, looking up at me adoringly! I felt all the more guilty for leaving her behind! Lizzy had serious separation issues and my leaving her did not help. She did not trust me now, to leave me out of her sight any more. I resolved not to leave her behind anymore. But that, as I soon found out, was easier said than done!

"Lets plan a trip to Europe!" my husband announced dramatically, the next year.

I stopped what I was doing, shocked! Abhishek looked up from his study books to see if the world had suddenly turned topsy-turvy, while he had had his nose in his books!

My husband grinned at our shocked expressions.

"No really. We have not had a luxury holiday after our cruise trip to Singapore. So why not go to Europe. I have not visited it."

"But I have lived there with my parents and seen all there is to see. Why not go some place else? How about only Scandinavia? I have not seen that," I countered.

"Oh c'mon Ma. We have not seen Europe. Only you have," my son protested.

"You guys can always see it when you go there from work, when you are all grown up," I reasoned.

"Ma! That's like eons later!" howled my sons.

"So its decided then. We'll book for Europe tour?" my husband asked for confirmation.

I looked dubiously at Lizzy. Then I looked up to see three pairs of eyes at me, staring derisively, waiting for my protests. I said nothing. My face said it all.

While my husband contacted the travel agent, he gave me the job of arranging the best tour. He also gave me the contact number of a friend of his who had recently been to Europe, so that I could find out a good schedule. I also had a pretty good memory of my teenage years in Europe with my parents and I painstakingly figured out a 15-day tour from among the offers given to me by the travel agent. This about covered the major tourist spots in Europe, without touching east Europe and Scandinavia.

I was now free to officially worry about Lizzy! 15 days was a really really long period in a dog's life, especially if you consider that one dog year is seven human years! I knew Lizzy would take it hard, particularly if she was left with strangers in a shelter.

I spoke to the same maid and asked her if she could squeeze in looking after Lizzy for 15 days. I promised her that I will pay her more than before if she devoted more time to Lizzy here at home and not leave her alone for long periods, now more than ever, since it was for a long period.

Even when that got settled, as the days passed and the day of our departure came closer, I was definitely uncomfortable with a strong sense of foreboding. I even told a friend and colleague of mine to keep calling up my maid and if possible, to come over home, and check up on her, and my baby, sometime.

Lizzy picked up on my panic waves and acted very strangely time to time, going off her favorite foods, even meat. She was vomiting more often and I was against medicating her. I had read somewhere that grated apple left to the air and on turning brown, was a very good remedy for gastritis. I tried it on Lizzy and it worked, both for her vomiting and loose stools.

I went over and over the details of Lizzy's feeding, her walking schedules, her intermittent bathroom breaks, the works, with my maid, as d-day approached. It was not a nice feeling to leave Lizzy behind. Lizzy was so attached to me and I felt so terribly guilty about leaving her all by herself for 2 weeks. Besides, like I said before, Lizzy had a major hang-up about separation.

We left very early in the morning, while it was still dark, as is common for all international flights. The maid had already come in, the night before, and was staying over, so that she could be here when we left and Lizzy was used to her at home while we disappeared.

I didn't want to say 'bye' and upset Lizzy further. So we left quietly. Loaded our luggage onto the cab and bid goodbye to the maid. Lizzy kept glancing at us, hopefully. I didn't meet her eyes. I had also left strict instructions to my sons not to say 'bye' to Lizzy and upset her.

I rang up at a decent morning hour from the airport. The maid informed me that Lizzy slept off after we left, but came willingly for the walk without much ado. After that, she was sitting quietly on the balcony without having her morning milk. In fact, she hadn't even smelled it. So there it was. Lizzy was declaring war on food because we deserted her!

"Oh, c'mon ma! Stop being so dramatic!" my sons chorused, when I informed them sadly.

'Yeah right. Poor Lizzy is suffering while are enjoying and I am being overly dramatic for you guys," I said sarcastically.

Although my cell picked up a signal when we landed in Italy, I didn't dare ring up coz I had tried messaging and I used up all my currency in two messages! I decided to wait for 2-3 days and call up from my husband's international sim card.

My colleague had replied to my messages saying that she had checked up with my maid, and Lizzy was definitely off her food but it was not all that bad. She was finishing up by dinner time!

And so it went on. Lizzy had more off days than good days and we just had to tolerate it. At least she was at home, in familiar surroundings, with a caretaker, who wasn't me but it was someone she was known to gel with, and who had been with her since her puppy days.

I did call a few times, and even tried conversing with Lizzy but apparently, her majesty did not approve of phone conversations because she walked away dis-interestedly! The phone lines over our mobile to the land-line in Bangalore was so clear. Kudos to modern technology!

Obviously, I had not bargained for the welcome that awaited me on my return. Lizzy sure knew how to keep my brows furrowed!

We returned in the afternoon late April. Bangalore had been lashed by rain the whole time we were away, so much so that our area had been inundated with water and many low-lying areas were still under! But the day we landed, it was a hot April day. Lizzy was sleeping off the heat when we rang the bell. I could hear her come up to the door and sniff vigorously. Then she started pawing the door. Then I realized that it was mid-afternoon and the maid would have gone. So I took the key from the security guard and opened the door.

It was then that I noticed that the mosquito meshing fixed onto the grill door was torn and hanging loose at the lower end. My heart skipped a beat! I had a feeling of dread as I stepped into the house!

Lizzy jumped at us with loud whines that were filled with protests!

"Why did you leave me and go? I was so lonely and upset! I was pining for you guys!"

I was too shell-shocked at the view that greeted us in the living room, to really pay attention to Lizzy's pitiable cries of joy.

The sofa was in tatters. The sponge was strewn all over the living room. The outer covering was in ribbons, some hanging to the main body by a mere thread! The main 3-seater one was so badly torn that it had no semblance to its original form. One of the single seater's had their front portion ripped apart, while the other one, amazingly, was intact! The sponge was being blown into every room by the overhead fan. The dining table chairs were overturned. Thankfully no damage was done to them.

As I stood there in horror, my mouth agape, Lizzy realized that people were not too happy to see her and her surroundings. She sat down on her haunches, tongue lolling and blinking her confusion.

My sons were waiting for my wrath to subside before they ventured any comment, to avoid getting caught in the crossfire!

I was actually too numb to react! I didn't even know such destruction could be brought about, let alone by such a sweetheart like Lizzy! I sat down on the only surviving sofa and contemplated the devastation, trying to collect my thoughts and deciding on a future course of action, while the one-animal demolition team run by Lizzy, stared back at me, perfectly still, wondering why nobody was running to her with sweet words of endearment.

"Lizzy, what did you do?" I cried softly. "Papa is so going to kill me!"

Lizzy knew that tone and the words 'what did you do' very well, and knew they did not mean well for her piece of mind. She licked her lips anxiously.

My sons decided they would keep out of this discussion!

"Lizzu . . . . how are you? What did you do all these days?" they cooed to her.

Lizzy jumped out of her reverie and raced across to them.

"Woof . . . . woof . . . . woof . . . . !" she replied and then cried plaintively.

"Poor Lizzy. All alone for so many days. Cho . . . . sad."

Lizzy jumped up and down.

"Be careful. You are just increasing the mess!" I barked.

I would not like to go into the details of the reaction of my husband and the grave consequences we had to face when he finally saw the annihilation of the sofas! Suffice to say that until we, read I, got the sofa repaired, we were all collectively grounded from any outings. Lizzy was in the proverbial dog-house for eons!

I wondered, in retrospect, how it could have happened since Lizzy is wont to create such havoc only if left alone for a very long time, especially the front door breakage. And since the maid was supposed to be with her at all times, except for an hour here and there, there was no way Lizzy could wreak such havoc unless, I suspected, she had been left unattended for hours.

I later came to know from the neighbors that in the initial days of our departure, the maid would dutifully stay as long as possible with Lizzy and close all the doors properly before leaving her inside the house. As the days went by, she got lazy and would only lock the netted door, leaving the wooden main door open. Obviously Lizzy, as is her habit, kept pawing on the netted door, finally tearing it.

The maid had also started leaving Lizzy alone for longer periods seeing that Lizzy was not doing any harm to the stuff inside. But Lizzy is like a time-bomb! She explodes when you least expect it!

So both the balcony door and the front netted doors had suffered casualties, the balcony door more than the front one. In fact, the balcony door net was coming out of its slot and would not get hammered in. So we just left it at that, repairing the front door net ourselves.

The day of our arrival, the maid had left Lizzy the whole morning all alone, thinking that anyway we would be coming and all would be ok! Lizzy got restless by mid-morning and tried pawing the front door net, getting more and more angry at it and doing irreparable damage.

She set her targets on the sofa next, wreaking devastation on it. This time, the casualties were the 3-seater sofa and one single seater. The 3-seater was badly mangled.

My daft maid laughed it off embarrassedly, not knowing what to say, admitting it was a mistake to take Lizzy so casually. I threatened lightheartedly that she would have to bear half the costs that I will incur in repairing the sofa. She certainly sat up at that!

Lizzy walked on tip-toes for a while after that. But her subservience did not last long! She was soon back to her brattish ways!

I came to know later that dogs with 'separation anxiety' tend to behave like this. Being kept away from their loved ones creates so much chaos within them that they go haywire! One cannot be angry and upset at passions evoked due to anxiety. This act was not vindictive.

Lizzy was so much loved by us that we forgave her but after this episode, she was banned from getting onto the sofa or getting familiar with the sofa! My husband would get furious if he saw her anywhere near the sofa! Lizzy would absentmindedly get on it at times, for which she was quickly reprimanded! For her the sofa was something that implied 'cozy' and which memory was firmly ingrained in her mind since childhood. But she soon realized that the sofa was an option only when the maid or the boys were around. With me too, she could afford to take lenience at times. But it was an absolute 'no-no' when my husband entered the house!

She looked so amazingly cute, cuddled up on the sofa that sometimes I didn't have the heart to chase her off! So I would ignore her furry form on the sofa but at the same time, I didn't want her to think that she can get away with murder! So I had to craftily avoid that area so that she doesn't realize I have seen her on the sofa and allowed it! Oh what a tangled web we weave!

She never did stop curling up onto the sofa. For her, it was a comfort zone associated with her growing up years and it implied safety and security for her. She didn't mean to disobey us. It was just instinct.

I repaired the settee under considerable cost to myself. The net doors on the front porch and the balcony, we somehow hammered it into place! It did look like somebody had bludgeoned it, but since it did keep the mosquitoes out, I did not give it much thought.

# (13)

## *Lizzy gets company!*

There were very few dogs in our neighborhood. We were, in fact, the first people to own a dog there and started the trend. Soon I saw a very furry dog in the apartment complex opposite ours. Turned out to be a golden retriever female with a very pleasant disposition. The owners were retired from the navy and owned the apartment they lived in.

Her name was Sunny, as in sunshine. She was a gorgeous golden brown furry dog, always playful, very friendly and very subservient to Lizzy. She came when Lizzy was already a full grown dog. So Lizzy made no bones of her seniority, from the first!

The first time we met was when the owners got her out for her small jobs. She saw Lizzy and tugged at her leash to meet her. Lizzy too ran over to her. Sunny immediately flopped to the ground, all four of her legs up in the air, in complete submission! Lizzy lost interest after that! She wanted someone rough and tough to challenge her, not a sweet little girlish fur ball! Sunny jumped onto me then and we had a lovely introduction. She was born to be loved and petted and crooned to.

We met Sunny on and off during her short walks by either the lady of the house or her grown up son. Sunny did not get to go on long walks and consequently, she did put on a lot of weight over the ensuing months.

I believe she was a very loved member in her family. She was never on leash inside her house and had the run of the house. I could see her from my bedroom window, noisily walking around the house, peeping into every room, inquisitively.

Her one favorite pastime was barking! She loved to keep barking all day long and at times, it was quite irritating. She had to bark at the birds twittering, at the local dogs fighting over a piece of bone, at the garbage van honking its arrival, even at the milkman delivering milk to the neighbor's! Staying across her and at a fair distance, her high-pitched continuous bark was mind numbingly irksome! I do not know how the immediate neighbors tolerated it, but I hear that there were no complaints. It would have quite a different story in our block!

If Sunny started barking, we knew there was no end to it, and that we were in it for the long haul! It happened in high intensity, only if she was let out in the balcony, probably insecurity or something. It only very occasionally happened when she was inside the house. But the incessant barking continued for as long as she was outside, even if the door was open and she had accessibility to the inside of the house. Sunny was only as good as her bark. She did not have a violent bone in her body and probably did not even know how to bite! She was full of love for every living thing.

Some days we were invited to let the dogs play up on their terrace. This was a welcome relief since Lizzy was not 'allowed' anymore on our terrace. So I took Lizzy up onto their terrace accompanied by a delirious and very bubbly Sunny. The terrace was rather small, compared to the one we had.

On seeing the open space, Lizzy bounded onto the terrace happily. Sunny followed suit. Lizzy took this as an invitation to play rough and tumble! She charged at Sunny, jumping on her unawares. Sunny cowered in submission, happily submitting her underbelly to Lizzy. We were all then greeted by the most deafening howl and screeches, like a million banshees dancing in hell! Turned out that a little girl in the group of children playing alongside, could scream the place down, giving ample competition to Sunny's high decibel barks!

To say we all jumped out of our collective skin, was putting it mildly! The howling continued for as long as Lizzy pinned Sunny down playfully, and was repeated with increasing decibel levels, each time Lizzy jumped Sunny! I gave up. Not only was Lizzy not playing and Sunny not enjoying the outing, but the bawling and wailing from the humans, was enough to set anybody's teeth on edge. I did try admonishing the tiny tots but to no permanent avail. It was horrible! I have a strong suspicion Sunny must have picked up her high decibel incessant barking habit from that human child!

Every day when Lizzy and I happened to play in the car park after the morning walk, if Sunny happened to pass by, she would whine next to the gate and wag her tail longingly. Lizzy, as is her wont, always jumped up to growl her displeasure at the intrusion! So the owner had to drag Sunny away. The days I reached Sunny first, brushing Lizzy aside, I just had to croon sweet nothings to her, setting of a tail wagging marathon by Sunny! She loved being petted.

One day, Lizzy and I were playing 'fetch' and I threw her coconut 'ball' a fair distance. Unfortunately, the coconut slipped through the gap underneath the gates and rolled outside. Lizzy, the madcap that she was, flew into a rage! She jumped a low lying wall alongside the gate, hurled down some 5 feet onto the road, to retrieve her precious 'ball', which she had impressively carted along during her walk for over a km! All this happened in a flash and I had just time to register Lizzy jump the wall and follow it up with some fierce growls!

Startled, I walked over to the gate and saw to my horror Lizzy baring her teeth at Sunny and stamping her paw firmly on the coconut! Apparently, the coconut had rolled onto the spot where Sunny had just sauntered onto. Smelling Lizzy's saliva all over it, Sunny playfully held it by her upper jaw, by which time, Lizzy was onto it like a flash and hence all the ensuing drama!

Promptly, Sunny rolled over in utter submission! Lizzy was not impressed. She still had her paw firmly on the 'ball' and was looking down at Sunny aggressively. Sunny's owner was tugging at her leash, but Sunny would have none of it. She saw an opportunity to meet more loving people, and she didn't want to budge from there!

Obviously I couldn't jump over the locked gates, not in front of an audience! So I sternly ordered Lizzy, "Lizzy wait. Stay there till I come, and no funny business."

Again, obviously, Lizzy did not understand my words! But she understood my tone of voice and could make out in her doggy mind that I was not happy with the turn of events, especially since I was required to go back home and get ready to go to work.

I raced around the garden, out of the gates of the apartment complex, and dashed into the road that lead to where all the drama was taking place. Thankfully, Lizzy was still immobile on the 'ball'. Sunny was up and about, a fair distance from Lizzy, just to be on the safer side. So was Sunny's owner! Lizzy was all lamb-like when she saw me thundering down the road! She kept wagging her teeny-tiny tail, tongue hanging out, but with her front paw still on the 'ball'!

Sunny jumped up on seeing me, her tail swishing in delight, dragging her human owner in her efforts to greet me! Lizzy growled warningly, seeing Sunny's attempts to move!

"Lizzy, stop bossing around!" I exclaimed, keeping a watchful eye on her majesty, and getting in between Lizzy and Sunny, in case Lizzy had any plans to jump her.

"Woof!" was Lizzy's agitated response. Her paw had not budged from the 'ball'!

"Ok Sunny baby. You are such a sweetheart," I crooned. I hugged Sunny, as she stood up to her full height and placed her front legs on my shoulder. I then, greeted her human owner, and then glared at Lizzy, as she lifted the 'ball' in her jaws and gave a low deep-throated growl again, looking side-long at Sunny.

"Lizzy, pick up the ball and lets go," I admonished, thinking it was best to make a getaway, before Lizzy stared getting bolder! "I am getting late, thanks to your pranks!"

Lizzy dutifully trotted along, with the 'ball' held firmly in her mouth. We entered the gates of the apartment without further incident. Soon after, Lizzy turned towards the garden to play some more!

"No Lizzy girl. We are going home. I am already late," I laughed. Lizzy just wanted to play the whole day.

I turned back to see Sunny also being led by her human owner into her home. She was still swishing her tail in obvious enjoyment of life!

Sunny got her cycles! Its messy in a dog because they don't sit still and obviously you cannot make them wear a diaper! To make matters worse, her owners had some relatives over and it was creating a delicate situation all around!

This I came to know when Sunny was being held downstairs on the road next to their apartment for her job by the lady of the house. She expressed her regrets about the whole matter. I helpfully suggested spaying Sunny so that this problem would be solved and the dog also benefitted. I also gave her the details of how to go about it and the story of my own experiences with Lizzy.

There was a visible look of delight on her face when she realized that there was a solution at hand for all the problems.

But sadly, they never actually got around to it, claiming lack of time!

One evening, I was returning from my evening grocery shopping, when I saw Sunny again, next to our apartment gate. Sunny was delighted to see me and made it very obvious, by going down on her back and submitting her belly to me. I scratched her belly while crooning sweet nothings to her.

"its very difficult to look after a dog at home," the owner remarked.

"No. it's a joy and I look forward to coming back every evening to be with Lizzy," I countered, surprised. I didn't know that they were having second thoughts about this beautiful, affectionate, loyal creature.

"Sunny is very active and its quite difficult to take her for her jobs frequently. There's nobody to play with her also."

"Well, young dogs are very active, and that's the whole joy of it. Its not nice to have a quiet, lazy dog around."

"Your sons play with Lizzy, so for you its not such a prob. We got the pup for my granddaughter. But she is too young to play with her or take her for walks. In fact, I am thinking of leaving Sunny in our farm, where there is plenty of running around space. But nobody dedicated to looking after her. Besides, my granddaughter cries when I say that."

"You could always give her away," I countered.

"Who will take a grown up dog?"

"Well, there are many organizations who will take her, if you can't look after her."

With that, I returned home thinking how unlucky some dogs are. Their owners just need excuses to give them away, a part of their families away. Where was the commitment, I thought forlornly.

Just out of curiosity, I put the matter on the table that night at dinner time, in front of my sons.

"How would you like to have another dog?"

"For ourselves? All the time?" queried my younger son, always enthusiastic about more animals.

Abhishek had a pensive look on his face. Undecided.

"Sunny's owners don't want to have her because they can't look after an energetic dog."

"Sunny! Ohh! She is so cute! Ma, lets take her ma, lets lets lets . . . ." screeched akhilesh.

"What do you say abhishek? Do you think we can handle 2 dogs? Walks and everything?" I asked.

"Yeah. Sure. I don't think its such a problem."

"And you guys will not mind taking 2 dogs for the walks?" I pressed on, making absolutely sure they knew the pitfalls.

They both felt it was not such a big deal and were happy that Lizzy would have a companion.

So it was that the next day when I met the owners of Sunny, I put the suggestion to them that if it was all right with them, I wouldn't mind adopting Sunny. The lady was delighted and promised to talk it over with her family before coming to a decision.

As expected, they gave up Sunny.

And so it was that a fully grown, golden retriever, came to be part of our family. Lizzy was already familiar with her but that did not stop her from telling Sunny in no uncertain terms that she was very low down in the hierarchy and needed to stay in her place! Sunny had absolutely no idea that she was with us for keeps. She had such a sunny disposition that she settled in with us happily, but kept looking at the door, expecting her owners to come back and fetch her. Although her tail never stopped wagging, especially when we were talking to her or petting her, she never stopped thinking about her owners, for the simple reason, during the evening walk, if she met her previous owners, she would tug at her leash to go to them.

Sunny was born to please! She never minded anything and whatever you did to her was just super in her world. She ate anything poured into her plate and usually licked it clean! This for me was like getting the pot of gold at the end of the rainbow! After being with fussy, high maintenance Lizzy her majesty the Queen, Sunny was a welcome delight! No fuss at all.

She was not used to being taken for long walks and the first few days, she would refuse to walk after the first 10 minutes! Especially so if we happened to walk in front of the apartment gates. She would stop in front and I had to drag her to continue the walk! And I could not train her to be left loose! Unlike Lizzy, she did not heed instructions! She just did not understand the tone and did as she pleased, which proved a bit dangerous! I was sure she would, like Lizzy, learn everything in time.

What really strained her back and tired her, was the games Lizzy and I played! She did attempt to chase the stick and the 'ball' a few times, but gave up after the second round. It gave her a shock when Lizzy charged at her with ferocity, at what-Lizzy-considered-*her*-ball! She squeaked in fright and immediately dropped on her back showing her vulnerable belly to Lizzy! So even though she was more than a match for Lizzy in size and weight, there was no competition as far as playing aggressively was concerned! Lizzy won that hands down!

And that's how the story unfolded!

I had previously discussed in detail with the owners, at the time of accepting Sunny into our house, that she needed to be kept away from her owners for the next 6 months at least, otherwise she would never really settle in with us and accept us as her owners. That was established to in spirit and I agreed to let them or their granddaughter visit Sunny after 6 months.

But what transpired on ground was entirely au contraire!

The granddaughter would screech in delight on seeing Sunny anytime, and even on spying her on the balcony, Sunny's name would be screamed and screamed! This agitated Sunny, who kept searching for the familiar voices she was hearing, to attach faces to them. I am sure she was mighty stressed on not finding the familiar voices attached to a body! Even during the walks, one of them, had to hug and fuss over Sunny. This way, I was in a fix as to how to get rid of Sunny's previous attachments and to get her to accept us totally.

I rang up the owners and conveyed my displeasure to them. Again, I was verbally re-assured that it would not happen again.

Obviously, that was not to be! My only course of action was to avoid going on that route which would entail my meeting with them, or to stop and return home on seeing them on my path.

Sunny, meanwhile, was enjoying her freedom immensely. What she was not really into was the long walks I was subjecting her to along with Lizzy! She looked longingly at the apartment gate each time we crossed it and stop momentarily, hoping I would turn around and enter the apartment! Then she started tugging at the leash, reminding me that home was here and not further down the road! She displayed marked reluctance to continue on long walks. This coupled with the vigorous game of throw and catch in our garage, resulted in her walking with a subtle limp.

I ignored it for a few days, thinking maybe it's the unusual exercise that was working new muscles. But the limp got worse and now she was noticeably not favoring her left hind leg. She stopped running after the 'ball' in the garage, waiting patiently till Lizzy got it, and then grabbing it playfully!

I took her to the vet then. He X-rayed the hip and diagnosed it as a mild form of hip dysplasia, common in such big dogs. He gave her some pills which I had to drop down her throat each morning.

I also asked him about spaying her and fixed an early appointment to do the same.

Sunny was an ideal patient. She behaved beautifully during and after surgery, which went off smoothly. Her post-op recovery was uneventful. I had to clean and re-apply her bandage each day, dressing the wound with iodine, and not once did she wince or whine, just sitting through it stoically. She placidly acquiesced to the cleaning and removal of slough. Even while I snipped the sutures off after 7 days, she never once turned her face or snapped at me. A model patient! She looked at me enquiringly once or twice, to ask if it was over and done with and hearing me say 'ok' was enough to get her on her feet, without a sound!

Unlike Lizzy, she did not bother with the dressing, not even trying to investigate what it was or gnawing at it to remove it. Lizzy was such a brat with the dressing! Sunny was back to her old self in no time!

With oral treatment continuing, her tolerance to long walks and vigorous play improved. She started enjoying the walks and forgot to tug at her leash on nearing the apartment gates. With her sweet mild disposition, it was a joy taking Lizzy and Sunny on the walks.

Of course, my avoiding her previous owners became a daily routine!

Matters came to a head one day in the morning when I was, as usual, in a tearing hurry to reach my work place. Sunny and Lizzy were sunning themselves on the balcony. There was a bit of a by-play between the owners and Sunny across the street. Sunny heard that and started a loud howl and vigorous wagging of her tail! I told them in no uncertain terms that their behavior was unwanted.

I received a visit in the evening. From the owners of Sunny. They did not take kindly to being told off. I asked her to back off in no uncertain terms. Then she started accusing me of not taking good care of Sunny and giving her 'step-motherly' treatment, by leaving her all by herself! The whole situation was so ridiculous! Here I was doing both her and Sunny a favor and I was getting tagged as the monster!

I laughed out at that point.

"You can take Sunny back if you want, and if you feel you can give her better care than me," I retorted, assuming that they would not do that.

"Ok. I will take her back tomorrow, after speaking with my husband. Anyway, my granddaughter, for whom we got the dog, is very upset we gave her away," that lady countered.

I was taken aback. But I had to agree.

The caliber of those people, specifically that lady, was made obvious the next day when she came back to take Sunny back, when she departed with the remark, "You have got her spayed also. So now nobody else wants to take her. We had another farm owner who wanted Sunny, but he wanted her babies. So he doesn't want to take her now!"

I was so shocked and speechless that I could not retort back! How commercial can people get! First she says her granddaughter wanted Sunny back. Then she says that she cannot give Sunny away because she can't get pups!!

And we call ourselves humans!

That beautiful, affectionate, loving and cheerful sweetheart had to go back to those people who wanted her pups and make a business out of it! How cruel!

I did give them all her X-rays and the medication. She commented that since Sunny did not have any hip trouble while she was with them, it must be because I had somehow induced it! I only hoped that the treatment would be continued and Sunny would be pain-free in her future.

Its not that I did not see Sunny after that. I got to meet her almost each day, being taken out for ultra short walks by that lady's son or husband, who were quite cordial.

Sunny appeared happy. That assuaged all my guilt feelings!

Sunny, for her part, accepted this phase in her life too. She remained effusive in her greeting towards us every time we met on the streets. Each time my car stopped next to her while she was on her evening walk, Sunny made it a point to pull on her leash and leap up on to my car window to greet me! She professed no ill-feeling toward me, for giving her up. Surprisingly, her demeanor had not changed a bit in all this exchange! She must have thought she was on a holiday while at our house!

Lizzy, for her part, did not miss Sunny! She wanted her mistress all to herself and did not believe in sharing! So as far as she was concerned, "good riddance" was what she felt! Although Sunny still greeted Lizzy as a long lost friend, each time they met on the streets, Lizzy was not effusive in her response!

My sons regretted my giving back Sunny! My younger son, akhilesh, was depressed about it for days, till I promised him we will get another dog from the pound to cover Sunny's absence. He insisted that I should have argued and resisted. But later accepted that I could not have done much since the owners believed I was treating Sunny badly!

# (14)

## *Dognap anyone?!*

I merely had to hint to Lizzy that I was planning to go to the bedroom, and before I knew it, she was off there, preceding me, out spread-eagled on my bed, rummaging the quilt to find a cozy spot! Since there's such a large area of her, I ultimately had to squeeze in somewhere in the left over space!!

Generally, Lizzy, considers my bed her domain! I find myself left out of the mattress area!

Lizzy first goes to the bed. And the manner in which she does it, is also so endearing! If she is sleepy, she'll just walk slowly, giving us sidelong glances to see if anybody is protesting at her advances, then trudge up to the bed, stop for a moment to contemplate the next action, and then jump up. She'll walk across the pillows next, tumble a few of them down so as to make a cozy spot between 2 pillows, for the length and breadth of her, and then spread herself parallel to the headstand, such that there are pillows on either side of her and she is nestled among them! She looks so contented and at peace that I am loath to disturb her at most times. Of course, my husband has no such compunctions!

Now, the scene shifts to when I am retiring to sleep. As I settle down on my side of the bed, Lizzy stands at the foot end, just raring to jump up! I have been caught unawares before, but now I am wiser! Earlier, she would jump up on to the bed, before I could settle in, and then spread herself all over the bed, such that I would be left with about half a foot space to squeeze in! I have tried pushing her, but boy, she is heavy and quite resistant to re-placement! So now, I keep warning her rather sternly not to jump up. Many times, she listens but there are times when the seriousness of my voice escapes her and Lizzy jumps up! Trying to outwit her requires a lot of planning and craftiness!

I first get up on the bed, pull the quilt aside, all the while saying 'NO' in a stern voice, and adjust my pillows. Then I get in, pull the quilt up and sigh contently. That's the only signal she needs! My sighing!

Lizzy will jump up, and land directly on your tummy, which if you are caught unawares, knocks the breath out of you, leaving you senseless for a few seconds! Lizzy feels she is only showing how much she adores you and will then proceed to lick your face thoroughly! That, is not something you need to be covered in just before you go off to sleep! And the more you protest, the more she feels you are encouraging it and will commence an even more vigorous slobbering on your face!

This stops, I learnt from experience, only if you rub her belly. Then she will close her eyes contently, licking her lips while she enjoys the belly rub, with her rump placed squarely on my midrib! The moment I stop her belly rub, she feels she needs to encourage me to continue, and she will proceed to give my face a second coating of her loving licks! I have to finally push her off unceremoniously to end the saga! She will then settle down on the other side of me, with her head on the pillow resting comfortably!

She changes her places of rest, many times while I sleep, ultimately going down to her mattress at the foot of my bed in the middle of the night, but I am totally unaware of it all. I only see her on her mattress curled up on herself in cozy comfort, lying contently in the morning.

But its God's truth, that she sure likes to unsettle me from my own bed!

Dogs, it seems, sleep for 16 to 18 hours a day, which is maximum in male dogs. Lizzy is a hyper-active dog at most times. But when she is content and secure, she sleeps. When she does that, I know she is not stressed. An un-stressed dog is a happy dog.

Its funny how she behaves when she sleeps deeply and dreams! Her lips twitch, her paws shake and many times I have heard her give low barks or whines! She must be dreaming about chasing a big dog and attacking it, all to save her human owner and then emerging victorious! She must be reveling in her courage and bravery!

Even in her deepest slumber, Lizzy is always on the alert for 2 things—the magic words 'bye-bye' and the inciting word 'cat'!

When uttered, Lizzy is prodded in to reality and is ready for fight or flight! Obviously, 'bye-bye' has her looking at us enquiringly as to when we were going to move. But the word 'cat' has her totally on the prowl, hair on the nape of her neck straight up, ears twitching, and low growls emerging out of her throat, as she trots, daintily sniffing the air to find the whereabouts of the offending animal!

Dogs are light sleepers at night. They also like to change places frequently. Lizzy epitomizes this! She constantly changes her position and her place of slumber all through the night! The pitter-patter of her feet as she explores new areas of rest, do not disturb me at all. In fact, I am not even aware that she is roaming around. But it irks my husband no end and he has threatened to throw her out of our bedroom countless times! The only thing saving Lizzy from being banished outside, is my perseverance in cajoling my husband!

Of course, I have woken up on a number of occasions to the loud protests of my husband at Lizzy's prowls as she makes her way out! Lizzy's reaction to the admonition is comical! She stops dead in her tracks, looks at the human spewing offensive tirades at her, apologetically, but still tiptoes out of the room in search of new pastures! She then heaves herself up over the living room sofa and sighs contently.

"She's up on the sofa again!" my husband protests crossly.

"Yeah ok. I'll wean her out of it eventually," I reply sleepily.

"Oh c'mon. Get her off it now, or you'll never get around it!"

Just to keep the peace and get some well deserved sleep, I have to scream at poor Lizzy, in the dead of the night!

"Lizzy! Get down!" I yell.

"Oh God! There's that noise of her feet again!" my husband groans, turning over and thumping the pillow over his head to drown the noise!

I merely grunt in slumber. Lizzy meanwhile slowly makes her way back to the room. She always stops at the foot end of the bed hoping to find permission and place to squeeze in on our bed, amidst the flailing legs and hands of her human owners! She seems to find our bed with its thick quilt vastly more cozy than her mattress!

"Lizzy, no!" warns my husband, ever vigilant to her sly opportunistic wiles! He heard the pitter-patter of her feet stop and guessed correctly what she was contemplating.

Lizzy then proceeds softly to her bed in resignation. She does not defy, although she takes full advantage of me when my husband is not around! She looks at me with those large brown eyes, half closed while I am completely mesmerized! She then does whatever she wants, while I look on indulgently. I do discipline her, but only in life-threatening situations!

Although I get up very early to finish my chores before leaving for work, Lizzy does not believe in waking up so early. She gets up only when she knows I am ready to finish up in the kitchen and go for the walk. She will come out of the room then. By which time, if my husband has not woken up, there is hell to pay, as he finds her walking around, disturbing him all over again!

Like all dogs, Lizzy too sleeps most of the daytime hours. But she has a specific pattern for when I am at home and when I am not!

When I am not at home, she sleeps continuously, only waking up every 3 hrs. when she has to be taken down for her bathroom sojourns. She usually chooses to sleep on our bed! That's what the maid has observed. The moment we are out of the house, she sits on the balcony soaking up the morning sun for a while. Then seeing no signs of my return, she makes her way inside.

Once inside, she beelines to the bedroom! Jumping up onto the well-made bed, she paws at the pillows, re-adjusts the quilt haphazardly, views her mess in great satisfaction, and then settles down with her head on one of the pillows! She continues like this, dreaming her dreams, uninterruptedly. I am always greeted by protests from the maid about the well-made bed being thoroughly spoilt by Lizzy and the fact that she has to make it again, before we enter the house! But lucky for Lizzy, the maid too likes dogs a lot!

A change in venue to the living room sofa is next on the agenda, once Lizzy comes back after emptying her bladder!

A long nap later, she retires to the bed again! Of course, once my maid sits down after all her work, Lizzy prefers to take a nap next to her, for some human company. This is till the boys come home from school, after which Lizzy often makes Abhishek's bed her own!

Abhishek always takes a short nap, before his busy evening schedule of sports and studies begin. Lizzy somehow manages to get onto his bed, in between his big torso, squeezing in anywhere between his pillows and the wall! She always supports her head on his leg and although Abhishek is tolerant and loathe to move so as to not disturb her, he does get a cramp in his hip as a result of being forced to sleep in one position only! Since he does not move at all, Lizzy finds it eminently restful and peaceful to lie there the whole time!

She does not extend the same courtesy to my younger son, Akhilesh, who is a very volatile sleeper, tossing and turning quite frequently with nary a care in the world! Many times, Lizzy has been either pushed off or kicked off his bed by his tossing and turning during sleep! Now she very discreetly prefers to cozy up to Abhishek!

The days I am at home, as on a holiday, Lizzy's sleep patterns are quite different! After the walk and her meal, Lizzy chooses to sleep in front of the kitchen, where I am working, so as to be ever vigilant about my movements, in case I should take it in my mind to escape her eagle eyes and flee the house without her! So eyes and ears on high alert, she lies spread-eagled on the kitchen mat, right at the entrance, so that even if her eyes and ears fail her, I would have to knock her over in trying to escape from the kitchen!

The constant noises from the kitchen re-assure her that I am still in action in the kitchen and her eyes remain tightly shut for the duration. As I get the breakfast table ready, Lizzy follows me like a hawk, from the kitchen to the dining table, back to the kitchen, till she is thoroughly disgusted at my repeated routine and will flop next to the breakfast table or under one of the chairs. She will lie there for the remainder of our breakfast, ever heedful to my movements. Then its back to the kitchen floor, up until I come out again for a cuppa. With a deep sigh of discontent at my restless habits, Lizzy occupies the sofa, curling up on herself.

I relax watching some TV, while Lizzy now settles into what appears to be a deep slumber. Inevitably as the TV is switched off and I start moving again, Lizzy's eyes flicker open and she watches me with half closed eyes. As I retire to my room for my bath, Lizzy slowly gets down from the safe comforts of the sofa. She stretches languidly, yawns a few times, and with a deep sigh again, follows me in. She then, will give me a look sleepily,

"C'mon, how long are you going to keep up this constant moving and unsettling me. I am not getting any rest you know!"

Mid-mornings are very lethargic for Lizzy. She does not have the energy or the mood to be active unless the subject really interests her, like a scrawny cat for instance! Failing that, Lizzy prefers to follow a specific sleep pattern, which involves a whole lot of resting and dreaming! Soon after entering my room, Lizzy has a very straightforward goal. To get comfortable on the bed! She does that and waits for me to get out of the bath, during which time she would have had vivid dreams of chasing dogs and cats and squirrels! Not so much about eating mutton or chewing bones!

The moment I leave the bedroom to sit on the living room settee, Lizzy will give one of her deep sighs again, and slowly walk across to me. After some much needed TLC, Lizzy chooses to either sunbathe in the balcony or curl up in the sofa, until otherwise told to move off!

The only time, she has ever been irritable and snapped at us, was during the time the anesthesia was wearing off after her surgery. At all other times, Lizzy has been the epitome of gentleness and love, even when disturbed during her slumber.

Happy and de-stressed dogs sleep peacefully. It follows that dogs which sleep well and fully are always happy and not under any stress. This is practically demonstrated by Lizzy, when she is with us in familiar place such as home, rather than in an unfamiliar strange place, even with us around. For instance, when we take her to Mysore, a city 130 km away, south of Bangalore, also known for its salubrious climate. My in-laws stay there. When we visit them, we drive down along with Lizzy.

The entire journey takes about 2 ½ to 3 hrs. house to house. Lizzy spends all that time in the car, sleeping! When we leave the city limits, Lizzy savors the outside breeze ruffling through her fur, ears flying back, eyes closed in abject contentment. In about 15 mnts., we see her comfortably stretched out and snoozing. Lizzy has never had car sickness, although while driving out of Mysore once, she did puke and bring out all the contents in the car and I had to stop and clean the whole mess.

But its actually a waste taking Lizzy for a drive. She solemnly sleeps! She spread-eagles herself languidly, with her head sometimes on the door handle, sometimes on the car seat, without a care as to whose place in the car she is nudging out! She maintains this position till half time, when I stop for a bathroom break for her. Then she comes wide awake, rearing to jump out of the car and do her job. Now Lizzy never has any problem keeping to the side of the road while she does her job, so I never have to put her on leash.

After the break, its back to sleep land! She keeps this up till we reach the outskirts of our destination, when I stop again for a bathroom break.

Since there is always another person in the rear of the car along with Lizzy, many a time we have seen her use their lap as a resting place for her head! There is something so cute and cuddly about having her face on one's lap that it becomes difficult to move so as to not to disturb her! Of course, she does not alter the position of her head even if one were to move a little!

Now Lizzy has been to my in-laws place since she was a little pup and she is quite familiar with it. But from the moment we step out of the car to enter their house, till we leave my in-laws house to go home, she will latch on to me and will follow me everywhere without being the least bit tired of getting up and lying down, getting up and lying down, time and time again! We have tried re-assuring her, comforting her, the works, but she insists on following me around like Mary's little lamb, not once letting me out of her sight. It seems very tiring for her by the looks of it, but Lizzy does not agree! Even when I am in the bathroom, she sits outside waiting patiently till I come out, not budging from her seat, come what may, however enticing any other offer is proffered. The only thing on her mind is to make sure I am there in her sights. She keeps this up every trip, even now when she is 5 yrs. old. She refuses to believe that we have all gathered just for a visit and will all go back together with her.

There's not much sleep she gets there, as a consequence. She's up and about almost all the time since I keep moving around the house. So the only time she gets any rest is when we are down for a siesta in the afternoon and retire for the night. That's just about 7-8 hrs. of sleep in a day, which cannot be good for a dog. But Lizzy is none the worse for it! She's just as enthusiastic about everything and everybody as always. As energetic and hyper active as she normally is. So I suppose she somehow rallies around the lack of sleep for those 3-4 days.

The worst of it is when we leave her at home with my in-laws and go out for a short spell to see the city or visit another relative. She does not close her eyes at all! My mother-in-law insists that Lizzy sits opposite the front door, watching it intently, on the alert for any movement or noise to herald my arrival. She does not sleep, does not drink water, does not eat, does not move at all from her vigilant position opposite the door! Of course, I feed her and make her drink water and take her for her jobs *before* going out anywhere. But still its heartrending to experience that kind of devotion and dependence.

I remember this New Year's eve one time. We had all gone for a dance party and left quite early in the evening. I had finished giving Lizzy her dinner and we had taken her for her night walk to help her finish her jobs. By the time we returned from the party, it was the wee hours of the next day. But Lizzy was seated right opposite the door, right where we left her! Her water bowl was untouched. The biscuits left for her were not even investigated! Although they were gobbled up the moment we entered the house!

She had never whined, never pawed at the door, never barked, never joined my in-laws into their room when they retired for the night, in fact, never moved an inch from her vigil opposite the front door! She just waited there, eyes locked on to the front door, waiting patiently for my return, knowing I would return to her, not doubting for an instant that I would not betray her! How can one not be affected by such abject devotion, such trust, such belief in your human owner. Lizzy did not sleep that night, not till we came back. But she was none the worse for it. She got up with us the next morning, enthusiastically waiting to be taken out for her morning walk.

She compensates for all this lack of sleep after returning home to Bangalore. She flops onto anything, her mattress, the kitchen mat, the front door mat, the clothes strewn around, our bed, anything, and then goes into deep sleep, not appearing for any meal, preferring to catch up on her beauty sleep. Even for her walks on those days, she is very reluctant to step out, choosing instead to rest and sleep. A true case of Lizzy-lag, as opposed to Jet lag!

# (15)

## *Conversing with Lizzy!*

**L**izzy is remarkably intelligent and savvy. She reads us well. We actually have not understood her language and mannerisms so well! She can make out by our tone, by some body odors that we emit, by our body posture, what we are asking of her, whether we are in a funny mood, angry with her, disapproving . . . . Whatever. She senses it and acts on it.

Bowwow . . . wow . . . wow . . . wowowowow . . . . !

That's how Lizzy's conversations begin! No half measures!

"Lizzy, come have your breakfast," I instruct her.

Lizzy looks quizzical. "Woof! Woof!" shaking her head! "I don't want breakfast!"

Now that is a response I am so familiar with! Eyes hooded, head bent low, 'tail' at half mast, slow steady steps towards me, stopping every now and then! Its her way of telling me, I don't want this breakfast, in fact, I don't want food. Lets get on with the walk and then we'll think about food! I am forced to come to you and I am uncomfortable.

She then comes within a foot of the food bowl and stops. Head still bent low, but eyes sneakily looking up at me, to find out what she's in for next. Is her human owner going to get angry and scream at her or just coax her to eat!

Now my reaction stems entirely as to whether I am within time or running late!

Hearing the warning tones in my voice, Lizzy licks the porridge bowl a little, looking up at me to say, "ok ok, I am eating. Just not liking it."

As a pup she was a lot less stubborn!

One time, I kept a beef jerky next to her breakfast bowl. The smell was very enticing. Lizzy had come right up to her bowl all on her own, sniffing the air curiously and liking what she smelt. I placed the jerky on the edge of her breakfast bowl and then took it out. She licked her breakfast, then hunted around for the delicious smell emanating, from somewhere! She looked up at me, licking her lips and waiting. I was supposed to understand that she could not connect the dots between the alluring smell and the bland breakfast! She licked some more thinking it was somewhere down below all the breakfast!

"Woof!" she suddenly bawled! I held the jerky away from her breakfast, allowing her to smell it and lick it but not get hold of it. And that's how she finished her breakfast and finally got to chew the jerky! I, the human, can also be as stubborn as her!

Dogs give funny looks when faced with a strange noises. Give a new squeaky toy to Lizzy and communication is endless!

I bought this large dumbbell shaped toy, which squeaked each time it was squeezed. Lizzy found that amazing! The first time I did it, she stopped dead in her tracks, ears twitching to find out the source of such a strange noise producing creature! She looked up at me, eyes wide open, the whites very prominent. She saw the peculiar toy in my hand making a bizarre noise . . . . and tilted her head very comically, first in one direction, and then in the other!

"Beep!"

Head tilt to the left, contemplate toy, stare at it and dare it to do again!

"Beep!"

Get startled. Head tilt to the right, glare at the odd creature, look up at human as if asking what's your take on this, give low deep-throated growl, keep head tilted to the right and glare more!

"Beeep!"

Head tilt to left and then right, and then jump at the toy! Lizzy did that absolutely silently!

She looked so quizzically comical that I was mesmerized, totally! I was completely unprepared for jump and grab routine!

"Woof! Woof! C'mon. Give it up! I need to smell and investigate this bizarre thing!" she yelped in frustration.

"You will destroy it in seconds. I need it to last. So keep looking only. No touching," I warned Lizzy.

Lizzy was not one to take no for an answer that easily.

"Woof! Woof, woooof, woooo . . . . ooof!"

She sat on her haunches and stared unblinkingly, first at the toy, then at me. If looks could kill . . . . !

I walked away slowly with the toy.

Lizzy tiptoed behind me, sniffing at my hands, as I juggled to keep the toy away from her.

"Woof, woof, woof, wooooooooofffff!" she cried.

"Ok, ok. But please make it last for at least 6 days, if not for the 6 months that the shop owner promised me!" I begged Lizzy, handing over the toy in defeat.

Lizzy grabbed the toy from my hands, and proceeded to tear it apart! Each time she applied pressure on it and it squeaked, she got angry and growled back at it! Finally getting totally exasperated, she held the toy in her jaws and gave it a vigorous shake, growling revenge! She got thoroughly rattled when the toy gave back an almost continuous squeak in response to the shaking! She dropped the toy and looked up at me!

I was in splits, holding my tummy in delirious laughter! Lizzy understood I was mocking her and lunged at the offending toy with her front legs. The moment her legs landed on the toy, it gave a loud squeak! To say Lizzy was stunned was putting it mildly! She was, in fact, too shocked to react immediately and stood with her legs on the toy, contemplating the rather continuous squeaks emanating from it!

"Grrrrrrrrrrrr . . . . ," she growled menacingly. The toy stopped squeaking. Feeling very pleased that she had subdued the strange 'creature', Lizzy picked it up and proceeded to investigate its parts!

Most of my acquaintances believe that dogs should be given professional training. I remember this working couple with 2 Labradors. They got a professional trainer to come in every evening to train their dogs. The jury is still out on debating the benefits vis-à-vis faults of professional training.

Personally, I do not believe in it. If you just spend time with your pet, speak to it as if it were a living being, which it is by the way, understand its reactions and tailor your instructions, it will get 'trained'. Why would you need to 'train' a loved one? All you need is for the said individual / pet to understand you and vice versa. Instinctively, animals do pay more attention to their owners voices, habits, routines and work themselves around it.

Lizzy was an able student in the school of understanding instructions. My sons always felt she was super intelligent. She understood us so well and so quickly.

Talking to her on the road while we took her for her walks, was enough to educate her in simple things.

"Lizzy, look, cat!"

That quickly taught her the name for her arch enemy! She not only understood 'cat' in many languages, but also picked up the nuances when we *spelt* it, to avoid making her go berserk! So any mention of 'C-A-T' would cause Lizzy to run amok, slipping on our house floor, growling and barking at the top of her voice!

'Squirrel'. That's another word she's picked up without my ever having to 'train' her! Each time she saw the offending animal, we yelled 'squirrel' and she latched onto that! Now all I have to do is mention squirrel out loud and Lizzy jumps over everything to race outside to spot a squirrel on the tree outside our house! Yes, she has associated squirrel with tree very smartly!

'Sit' is something I had to work on. We had to push her rump down and help her associate that with 'sit'! All we had to do was to keep repeating it each time we played with her. But we don't regularly get her to do it, because I don't see any reason for getting her to do it, unless I have visitors home and I require her to be in one place while the guests are settling down.

I didn't think of it as 'training' per se. All we did was keep using it while we were out walking with her or playing on the terrace with her, or even just playing a good old game of 'tug-of-war' inside the house.

"Lizzy stop! Don't cross the road till I tell you!"

Initially Lizzy just stopped because of the sense of urgency in my voice. I was desperate because there was traffic coming in from all directions. She stopped right at the edge of the road, looked up at me quizzically, and not finding me moving, did the same! She sat down on her haunches and waited patiently, while her owner did crazy things in the middle of the walk, like looking in all directions for some animal to descend upon!

"Ok Lizzy, we can cross now."

"I could have told you that a while back. See, I can smell if there's an animal around, with this thing called nose," she seemed to say each time, giving me an exasperated look.

For all that, Lizzy has no fear of anything, not human, definitely not human, not animal, not traffic. She just blindly assumes, everybody is there in this world to love her! Her act of not fearing traffic is most worrisome. Unless I give specific instructions, she merely skips her way through everything! Even a huge truck coming hurtling down does not put the fear of God into her. Like my maid says, when on a leash, and not receiving any instructions, Lizzy will take that opportune moment to pee in the middle of the road while crossing it, exactly when there's a large bus or truck careening down the road straight at her! Unfortunately, even that does not scare her! But it sure scares the living daylights out of my poor maid! I wonder what must be going on in her doggy brain—that a large gigantic creature with multiple odors is coming to pet her and spoil her silly!

Like all animals, Lizzy too finds disgusting items on the road absolutely delightful! Her nose is assailed by the aromas tickling her senses, the dirtier for us, the better for her! So the first thing I insisted on her learning is "drop it"!

As soon as she picked up the piece of discarded bone and decided to make a hearty meal of it, I said "Lizzy drop it right now!"

She soon comprehended that, especially when she saw me hurtling down the road with my hand raised a couple of times! Initially, when she didn't quite get the message, I had to come home and punish her by keeping her outside the house in the balcony. Now the one thing Lizzy hates above all, is to be left alone, away from company, and especially in a confined area, although it is open to the outside world! She does not like being restrained away from us. So that was an apt punishment for her. One that worked faster as a deterrent for her than any raised hand or stick would!

Each time she came back from the walk and had done something naughty, like gobbled up a piece of decaying bone or meat piece, or smelled some stool on the road, sneakily, before I could caution her against it, Lizzy was punished by being kept on the balcony till my departure to hospital, not allowed to mix with us. Oh boy! She so hated that! The balcony door bears so many scratches and bite marks as testimony to her frustration at not being allowed inside! Her barks and whines have reverberated throughout the neighborhood! But she got the message loud and clear!

The problem was the furtiveness with which she continued her bad habits after that! I had to be ever vigilant on the road with her! But Lizzy is an open book, if one only pays attention to her expressions and behavior! She has this classical guilty look on her face when she is about to do something she knows she's not allowed to do! Since she's never on leash and has a free run of the road / footpath, her nose is always looking for new smells down and the moment she finds something 'interesting', her web of deceit starts!

She looks back to see how far back I am and how much damage I can do to her before she commits the offense! She sniffs at the offensive item, all the while looking at my approach through the corner of her eyes! If she sees me hurrying up to catch up to her and screaming profanities all the while, she quickly picks up the titbit in her mouth and gallops away at top speed to outrun me! She may or may not drop it in a little while, depending on how serious she thinks I am!

So I have learnt to pick up on her body mannerisms. The moment I see her spending an extra amount of time investigating something on the ground, I warn her sternly, even from a distance. If she has just put it into her mouth, I scream "drop it Lizzy!" Most times, she drops it!

Lizzy loves playing! She is such a childlike, enthusiastic, whole-hearted creature, that for her life is one big playground and everybody around is only there for her majesty's amusement! She will pick up a stick or a coconut shell fallen by the side of the road, and yell at you!

"Woof! Woof! C'mon lets make this interesting!"

I am supposed to understand from her stance and bark that she's inviting you to play with her! She is relentless in getting around you! First she will pick up the stick in her jaws and prance in front of you! If you don't get the message, she will drop the stick and look up at you questioningly.

"Woof! Lets's play folks!"

If you continue walking ahead, Lizzy will gambol up to you, block your path and say "Woof, woof!"

Then she will run back, get the stick and frolic enticingly in front of you, till you have to resign yourself to your fate and play with her!

As I grab the stick still held firmly in her jaws, Lizzy will growl and pull back with all her might. Then I move away in mock anger.

"Woof. Ok sorry. I didn't know you had no strength!"

She will drop the stick in front of you. I pick it up and throw it as far as possible. Lizzy darts behind the flying stick. She will pick it up and bring it up to you again, expecting you to continue the game!

I did not train or teach her to understand "Lizzy, go pick up your ball." She taught herself that all on her own. If she has dropped her 'ball' and we have travelled some distance away, I just need to stop, look at her and give her that instruction. Lizzy is out in a flash, sniffing the ground to find out where she had last dropped her 'ball'! She will find it out and bring it to me triumphantly!

It's the same when we go up to the terrace to play. If her original 'ball' is not there, I instruct her, "Lizzy go get your ball."

"Woof! Woof!" she retorts.

"Lizzy go get your ball from downstairs."

This time, she will run down, search for the ball which she wants among the various contraptions she has collected over the months, and bring out the latest 'ball' she had picked up on the walk that morning and race up the stairs, 3 steps at a time, and jubilantly produce the 'ball' in front of me!

I had never taught the word 'Stay' to her. But I've used it on a number of occasions and Lizzy has followed it to the 'T'.

I remember the time when one day at the fag end of our walk, Lizzy being in high spirits still, due to the lovely cool weather we'd been experiencing of late, scampered after a squirrel she managed to spot across the road on a tree! How she managed to see a tiny tiny squirrel, brown in color, scurrying up a tree bark brown in color, is beyond me! But she did!

For a second, my heart was in my mouth as I imagined all kinds of serious accidents taking place at that instant, in all of which the end result for Lizzy was not very healthy! My logical brain stopped working! My reflexes took over! I realized Lizzy was planning to cross the road, back to me, and I could not allow that as the morning traffic, which included large school buses, was starting to rush along the road!

I screamed 'STAY' at the top of my voice, hoping with every breath in my being that Lizzy would not dare to cross the road back to me, against her instincts! She didn't! She did not look half as serious or involved as I wanted her to, in order to follow my instructions, which was not very re-assuring! She kept looking at me, at the tree for the squirrel, and at the hurtling traffic along the road! And she sat down on her haunches on the edge of the road, absolutely still, waiting for her human owner to cross over to her! Trusting her human owner to know the best and do the best for her, she paused there patiently, for what seemed like an eternity to me! I crossed over hurriedly in case she had second thoughts about waiting for me! I got down to her side and just hugged her in gratitude for listening to me!

I had used the instruction 'stay' earlier on a number of occasions! But never before that instant, did it assume such significance! After that, 'stay' has become something I use very often to get her to stop in her tracks and she obeys perfectly. Formal training or not, just bonding with your pet will give them the confidence to obey you and follow your instructions.

I remember another occasion, when I was completely unwell with a stomach bug which was causing me endless bouts of nausea and enteritis. I was off from work and laid up on bed with severe weakness. I still took Lizzy for her morning walk because nobody else could make the time. My sons had a school time to keep up to and I could not ask of them. Lizzy could not be denied her walk since she had to do her jobs.

Lizzy somehow understood I was very weak and stuck close to me all through the short walk. She did not stray far from me, did not run amok behind rats and squirrels, listened to my instructions even when I spoke in a very soft voice, because I didn't have the strength to even raise my voice, and behaved like a thorough lady! Wish there were more days like that!

She very conveniently finished all her jobs very early in the walk that day, so that I could return home and flop on the bed. There was no demand to play ball that day, and even Lizzy was very subdued. But what is so amazing and incredible is that there was a tacit communication that things were not normal and all her normal energetic state just dissipated in support of weak me. We did not need a spoken conversation with her to let her know anything. Such is the power of love and empathy, and a sixth sense that animals seem to possess. No human being would have such a tacit unspoken understanding with another human being!

I had her on leash that day because I did not have the confidence in myself to follow her without her leash on. Most days, Lizzy on a leash, is a very powerful dog pulling its human almost to a run, not a walk! Besides Lizzy's energy is almost always very high and she works it out on her walks, impatient to explore. But that day, she was as sedate as a kitten! She waited patiently while I walked with measured steps so that I don't fall en route. She kept looking back at me, waiting, asking if she was doing ok by me! I was so thankful to her that I had tears in my eyes. That's the power of communication with a loved one. That's an unspoken connection that comes in good stead in times of need.

The time my elder son, Abhishek, was very sick for over a month, Lizzy comforted him in a way only a dog can, and she was less than a year old! She wouldn't leave his side and for a while I was worried she would pick up his fever. She kept vigil day and night. He slept on the living room settee during day time and Lizzy, being so tiny and all legs only, somehow managed to squeeze in on the settee amidst his legs! He could not fidget because Lizzy was positioned very strategically across him, and she did not move at all so as to not disturb him! How's that for empathy!

There she slept however uncomfortable she was. Abhishek was glad for the company since there was nobody at home except the maid. I only managed to get some time off from work after 3 pm. Even though he was spiking temperatures, and his body was boiling, Lizzy did not leave his side. She was such a loyal mate in his hour of need.

When his temperature broke and he woke up, Lizzy licked him to let him know he was not alone! Even after I came home, she greeted me and then immediately trotted back to her allotted place next to Abhishek. She kept this up for over 3 weeks, till abhishek was out of the woods! How did she know he needed some warmth and contact with a warm blooded person? She just followed her instincts. She didn't care how uncomfortable she was. Her only thought was to give him security! Yeah, she was his security blanket! On occasions, I have woken up in the morning to see Lizzy cozily wrapped around Abhishek! She had obviously spent the whole night next to him. This was only during these 3 weeks. She did not ever go back and sleep with him at night after he became fit and healthy. How did she know? Uncanny huh!

# (16)

## *Crowd puller!*

A walk in the city's park. Lizzy was busy chasing all the squirrels, some imaginary. Anything that moved was eyed very suspiciously by Lizzy. She chose to ignore all the people trying to get her attention to cuddle her and instead faced the park and tree area, closely observing for squirrels! So many people took photographs of her. Apart from the constant barking, she behaved impeccably.

We started walking briskly and Lizzy was eager to move on. I had to have her on leash all through. She found plenty of rough patches by the side of the main road to leave a little bit of evidence of body fluids along the way! When we turned inside the Park, there was a wide stretch of green grass and a small gate with a pathway. I couldn't resist! So I broke off from the walk for a while and diverted with Lizzy into the green grass. I left her loose and she went bananas! Lizzy ran amok, enjoying the wide expanse and the freedom to exercise her long limbs.

Soon there was a crowd outside the boundary of the green expanse. People, morning walkers, were stopping and watching Lizzy run like the wind and catch pretend flies! She was bounding over the grass and then leaping out of it, jumping high in the air to 'catch' the offending fly! People were clapping as she sprung up into the air! Lizzy was in her element! She played to her audience to the hilt! Soon she accompanied her pole vaults with enthusiastic barking! That sent the crowd into raptures! It was as if a film shooting was going on! In fact, when we eventually came out, I had people ask me if indeed a film shooting on the dog was going on!

When Lizzy went berserk, she really did go nuts! She had this peculiarly adorable habit of tucking her hind legs in, such that they came very close to her front limbs, when she was doing super-sonic speeds! Of course, she had trouble stopping in her tracks after that! But she could turn even at those high speeds, in a wide curve and not reduce speeds at all! She looked like a powerful Ferrari zooming away! Except for the fact that she had a wide smile on her cute face and her tongue was hanging out of the side of her jaw, she could be mistaken for a modern space-age 2-seater vehicle, clipping mach speeds!

Everyone wanted to capture Lizzy on their mobile cameras. I was considering charging a royalty for the photographs! Lizzy was such a sweetheart about it that she let people, complete strangers, come sit next to her, keep their faces alongside hers and click photos, with an accompanying lick of thank you at the end of it all! All the enthusiasts were amazed at her gentleness and friendliness! She just loved people and didn't mind anything they asked of her! She just did not believe that they would harm her. Of course, I was by her side the whole time. She was not on leash but she knew I was around her and would protect her.

I eventually continued the walk and with the fast pace maintained by Lizzy, we did manage to reach the main entrance. Even after her marathon, Lizzy was not in the least bit tired! She was so curious and elated at the same time, to explore new smells, new animals and take in the fresh air. She did not want to turn back home. But by then it had already started getting a little warm. The sun was up in the sky and I was already getting tired of all the demands on Lizzy. Lizzy, of course, was reveling in her role as a star!

Breakfast was available nearby. There was a small stretch of grassy ground where we stationed ourselves while we had breakfast. I took the leash off and Lizzy had the run of the park area. She kept her nose to the ground hunting for new smells. I kept an eagle eye on her in case she decided to taste some offensive item off the ground! Lizzy also kept a wary eye on me and measured my distance accurately. The moment I got too close, she teasingly scampered off! The local vendors now started collecting around, to watch this show! Each time Lizzy escaped my clutches and danced away, a small applause greeted her! And she played the crowd, gamboling on the ground, clutching a stick and playing catch with it! So much so that here too, people started coming forward to take photos of Lizzy and themselves! I had to hold on to her harness while they played with Lizzy and took their photos, otherwise she was not keeping still at all. In spite of all that vigorous workouts on the grass earlier, she still had so much energy and stamina left!

I tried feeding her some tit-bits from the breakfast tray, a typical south Indian fare. But she would have none of it. Some people from the adoring crowd around her managed to produce some biscuits, which she gobbled up in record time! This again was a source of immense amusement and amazement to the locals! Soon people gathered with delicate snacks, vying for her attention, jostling with each other in trying to get Lizzy to take what they had to offer! Lizzy did total justice to their adulation, taking all the pieces from each individual and delicately chewing it, with a very thoughtful expression on her doggie face!

I excused Lizzy from the hands of the crowd. Eating that many unknowns would definitely play havoc with her tummy, I was sure. Lizzy, the drama queen, reluctantly tore herself away from the crowd! But she still hung back, hoping we could stay a while longer in this open expanse. But I was in a hurry to get home, even though it was a holiday for me. I still had chores at home.

"Ok bye Lizzy. You stay here," I said, rather indignantly, seeing her linger on. I then turned to leave the venue with my family in toe. Lizzy sat on her haunches. She looked at our departing backs, and at the proffered sweet meats from the people in front of her. Choosing wisely, she galloped behind us, accompanied by loud claps from the mass collected there!

It was obvious that although she enjoyed the outing, she was still glad to be back to familiar home turf and smell the accustomed odors around our house after the long walk. But it certainly was a revelation for me, finding out what a show off Lizzy was, and how much of a crowd puller she could be!

Lizzy attracted attention even during her normal walks. She was just so sweet natured around humans and so friendly and had such a pleasant expression on her face that people just loved her!

"Do you have any puppies of her?" is the oft repeated query during the walks, which even my maid says people have asked of her!

"No, no. I don't want to. She has been operated upon," I inform them.

I know Lizzy has such a pleasant disposition that her pups would have been dazzling! Besides of course, being absolutely cute, as only puppies can be! It would also not have been any problem giving them away. The problem was to search for good homes. My experience with humans having dogs, has been rather negative. Like I have repeatedly mentioned, dogs are not reared as family in our culture and in many places overseas, and people treat them rather dismally. So I did not want to have to be constantly worried as to how Lizzy's pups were being reared. Whether they were always tied outside, whether they were not loved like family and so on. So I refused to cater to the pup industry.

Our daily morning walks passed through a side-walk, in front of a large electronic showroom, which was also a school bus pick-up point. A few kids with their parents wait there for their school bus. The first time they saw Lizzy, the little girls there started fussing over her!

"How cute! Cho chweet!" accompanied by slurping kisses!

Lizzy did not need a second invitation! She ran upto them and tried to lick them! Seeing a large dog come sprinting at you, however friendly, is not the most pleasant scene, if you don't know the dog! So there was a whole lot of shrieking and screaming, which thoroughly confused Lizzy!

"Lizzy wait! Hold on! Go easy!" I tried calming her down.

Lizzy looked at me and then at the kids. She was rearing to have a go at them, but the urgency in my voice and the loud yelling stopped her in her tracks.

"Lizzy come back here. Go slow," I said softly.

"Aunty, will she bite?" the girls asked me plaintively.

"Lizzy is the gentlest of souls," I replied with a smile.

As if to prove my words, Lizzy slowly walked up to them and licked their extended hands.

"So cute. So nice to have a dog. Lizzy come here."

"No, Lizzy, come here!" Lizzy was getting petted by everybody there and reveling in it!

"Aw, no Lizzy. I have to go to school!" yelped a girl, as Lizzy tried to jump up to lick her and place her paws on her shoulder.

Meanwhile, some of the parents got into the act. There was general admiration for friendly Lizzy.

"We had a dog too, a puppy," one of them said. "He died in 10 days and we didn't know why. After that we didn't get another pet."

I duly sympathized, but my attention was all on Lizzy in case she got very excited and gleeful and frightened the young kids there. In her enthusiasm, Lizzy will try and go for the face to express her love for the human and I was not sure, these kids were ready for it as yet!

"Lizzy, enough! Come back. Lets go," I called out.

"Woof!" Lizzy barked back. "C'mon, I am so loved here. Let me play," She seemed to say.

"Lizzy. Come here. We'll meet them again tomorrow," I said sternly.

"Bye Lizzy. See you again," they called out.

Lizzy gave them a parting lick and then joined me on the walk.

Journeying by car with Lizzy is a delight, when her majesty keeps awake ie! Whenever we stop, she peeps out of the window. Depending on the weather outside, she will be active and pop her face out or lean on the window frame lazily if its hot outside, tongue lolling. Whatever the pose, its sure to get attention!

Dogs in cars are still an unusual sight in India. People don't prefer animals in their vehicles so that they don't have to clean up the fallen fur afterward.

So Lizzy at the window generates a lot of attention!

Once on a particularly hot day, the AC inside the car was on full blast, so all the windows were closed. Lizzy was sleeping inside as usual, but the wait at the traffic lights was a particularly long one. Lizzy's slumber was disturbed. So she got up lethargically and leaned against the window frame. She peered out to catch the view, with a vacant look on her face.

"Good God! That's a dog right there!" the driver in the adjacent car yelped, on suddenly seeing this huge visage next to him, only a foot away! His window was open, so for him, it was a sudden shock!

"Oh so cute! Aw . . . . Can we pet him papa?" came the cries from the rear seat of the car.

Lizzy's ears twitched and her tail started its miniscule movement from side to side! I looked back from the driver's seat and smiled at the neighbors. Getting over his initial shock, the driver of that car smiled back at us.

I rolled Lizzy's window down.

There were more shrieks of delight from the rear seat of the adjacent car.

Lizzy licked her lips.

"Lizzy. Go easy. No jumping and no trying to get to their face," I warned Lizzy in a low voice, menacingly.

Lizzy leaned out and allowed the kids in that car to pet her and fondle her. Thankfully, she did not try and jump out or try to get into the other car! But alas, she desperately tried to lick them, and she did succeed in licking their hands!

There were squeals of delight as Lizzy's warm licks caressed their skin. Children are so forthright and open, unlike adults.

Lizzy, the incorrigible, finally has to put me to shame! She put one paw on the window leaned into the driver, thrusting her face right onto his! He swerved just in time to avoid her tongue from giving him a white wash!

"Yeow . . . . !"

"Lizzy!"

We screamed in unison!

Lizzy retreated back, job not fully accomplished!

She looked back at me innocently.

"Sorry," I apologized to the driver, looking shame-faced.

"Its ok. I was just not expecting that and it was a shock," he smiled.

"How old is she? Does she have any pups?"

I laughed. "She's 1 ½ yrs. and no, I have spayed her, so no pups."

Lizzy, hearing me laugh, assumed everything was forgotten and forgiven! She put her paws on the window again and stretched her neck to be more accessible to the kids at the back. She joyously propped herself across the window, dying to make friends! The more the merrier! Her whole body started wagging, starting from the stump of a tail right between the shoulder blades!

The family across was mesmerized with Lizzy's antics!

"Woof! Let's play!" Lizzy suddenly barked.

"Mama, lets take her home!" the kids begged.

The light soon turned green.

"Lizzy sit. I am leaving now," I instructed urgently, in case Lizzy got caught between the 2 cars.

My sons joined me in ordering Lizzy to sit, and she did, thankfully, just as we moved forward.

"Bye Lizzy," the kids sang out to her.

Lizzy responded by wagging her tail and licking her lips.

Generally, evening times are spent lazing on the balcony. As I sit on the floor, my cell next to me, essential reading material alongside, my glasses in their case also brought for use soon, Lizzy takes that moment to want to play!

She dove headlong through the doggie door, along with her favorite chew toy of the moment and demanded that I play with her! Her play is usually very vigorous. She has been known to gnaw through hard wood in a matter of minutes! So one cannot take her invitation casually.

She thrust the toy onto my face, accompanied by growls and barks and pawing! Then commenced a very vocal game of pull-throw-snap-growl-hide-bark-paw in which I ended up with plenty of scratch marks! It also made for a very irritated Lizzy since she did not get an upper hand! Lizzy believes she is superior to her human when rough and tough play is on and it frustrates her no end when I outwit her! I have to give in many times in mock defeat just to get her to wag her tail in triumph! Otherwise, she turns her back on me in a huff, refusing to look at me for what she considers underhand means of not-letting-me-have-the-ball! This is especially so when I play hide-and-seek with the said toy around my back, tempting her to search around me to retrieve it!

Since patience is not a virtue in this family, Lizzy included, if the hide-and-seek-the-toy-behind-my-back goes on for a while, Lizzy will just sit on her haunches looking at me, panting, with a not very pleasant expression on her face! If I still do not hand the toy over to her in a platter, she will leave my side, go sit on the sill, back to me, showing her displeasure very obviously, at my not giving her the toy by what she considers fair and square!

The first time this was going on, I did not realize there was an adoring crowd looking at boxing bouts between man and animal and obviously rooting for the said animal! Little and big school kids were gawking askance at the fight put up by a very angry Lizzy! Since we live on the top floor and the balcony faces the main road, all going-ons are easily visible from a distance below. The house is at a cross road, so the number of ooglers doubles! Each time Lizzy won a bout, there was cheering and clapping! This was all the goading Lizzy needed to double her efforts to pry the toy out of me! The intensity of her attacks were directly proportional to the number of fans rooting for her, like a typical boxer in the ring! Boy! Lizzy took her bouts very seriously indeed!

The times I give the toy back to her in mock defeat, as in pretend-she-got-it-out-of-me in the fight which I was too weak to win, she will take the toy as far away from me as possible, in full view of the admiring crowd, carefully facing them so that they don't lose sight of her 'winning'! One other thing, if by any chance Lizzy feels that I 'gave' up the fight to let her win the toy, she will drop the toy down at my feet! She does not like to be given a win, she likes to fight for a win, or at least think she did!

There she will sit, facing the crowd, holding the toy between her front paws, eyeing them through the corner of her eyes, nibbling the toy for their benefit! Just to keep the interest of her indulgent crowd, she will come back inside for a return bout! That would be exactly when I am in the middle of an interesting read and do not want to take my eyes away from the book! But Lizzy, being oh-Lizzy, needs to have her way! So the rigmarole of repeat bouts get underway! This will go on till twilight sets in and it gets too dark for the adoring crowd to see anything and they start dissipating in ones and twos! Then Lizzy will lose interest in the toy and retreat to her favorite place on the balcony sill, savoring the view outside!

# (17)

## *The big bang theory!*

I used to love diwali or the festival of lights. But now, I dread it!

After becoming an animal lover and activist, I hate anything that brings anxiety and despair to animals. Loud noises and continuous noises that creates fear psychosis in the animals is reprehensible. Sadly, Diwali has now officially become the festival of noise, not so the festival of lights! With increasing population and innovative crackers, the decibel levels are mind boggling! And the noise lasts for 2 whole days!

We, as a community, have no regard for anyone other than ourselves. But then, we do not have any concern for each other as well, since we lack basic humanity. So how can it be expected of us to have any care for creatures less fortunate than us.

All animals hate noise and especially noise with such high decibel levels, creates immense anxiety in them. They override the fear by skulking or barking.

Lizzy, greeted her first Diwali with shocked terror! She was just 6 months old. She was so petrified, that she dived underneath the bed and refused to come out or eat! She developed a high temperature and was sick for nearly 5 days, refusing feeds and refusing all outdoor activity, including walks, which she normally so loves, during the whole time. At that point of time, I didn't know whether to get involved in the celebrations with my family or hold Lizzy close to me to comfort her. Obviously, the latter prevailed. I had to hold her completely enclosed in my arms.

To top it all, she barked incessantly, not even pausing to take a breath!

I could feel her trembling in fright, shivering with trepidation. She kept looking up at my face, and then diving into the crook of my arms. It was all I could do to comfort her. With every loud sound, she jumped out of her skin. No amount of coaxing made her eat. Even meat based food was smelt and refused. She stuck close to my legs during her walks. I had to drag her leash to go forward and she dragged it back with equal vigor! Finally, I took her in my arms for some distance. When we cleared our house area, I let her down and she agreed to walk, albeit, very subdued, looking up at me every now and then. She was so tiny and so helpless, and so frightened! I just wanted to pick her up, cuddle her up in to my arms, and hide her from the noises, inside my coat.

As she grew older, she responded to her anxiety by going on the offensive! She continuously barked at each bomb that exploded, to the extent that by the end of the 2 days of Diwali, she had a horribly hoarse throat! She lapped up water all the time, and obviously, what goes in, has to come out! Her bathroom breaks increased plenty!

She was so offended by the noise that if she saw a cracker, she connected the sound to the offending item and she lunged at it and tried to bite it! The first time she did that, we were caught unawares and the cracker flame singed her lips! Poor thing, kept licking her lips for 48 hrs.!

Now we are on guard if Lizzy's on the prowl! But even then, restraining her proves to be a herculean task! Its not just agitation, its as if her heart and soul are hell bent on catching the offensive item and destroying it, with a single minded devotion, defying all reasoning and logic and consequences! Its as if her life depended on it! She is deaf to all soothing words and resists all efforts to calm her down. She is that focused on the cracker! By the end of it all, she is frothing around the mouth and her heart is racing as if she has just run a marathon!

Diwali is the time, that I never leave Lizzy alone. My husband was totally against that rule! He wanted to visit relatives, leaving Lizzy behind. I was aghast the first time he suggested it! Ever since, we agree to disagree!

The point is Lizzy trusts us. She depends on us for protecting her, and this was her time of need, when she was the most afraid and tried to mask it by false bravado. All her bravado would probably disappear if we were not around and she would be shivering in fright!

The 3 of us, my sons and I, we are always apprehensive as Diwali approaches. As the sound of bombs start, Lizzy gets broody. She is off her feeds. She keeps looking at us for re-assurances. But however much we console her, she is driven by some insane need to bark continuously at the bursting of bombs. Each time she keeps up this tirade against the noise, I feel anxious and sorry for her.

The good part is that once the noise stops, Lizzy is back to her old daft self!

One year, we drove down to my in-laws place to spend Diwali there. Since I would not leave Lizzy behind, my husband spent the entire journey in stoic silence! Lizzy did not understand human politics and she happily went to sleep once we were out of the city limits and the stops were infrequent.

Lizzy was glad to stretch her legs once we got down. After thoroughly inspecting the premises, she settled down in the middle of the living room, right in the middle of the entire family now seated on the living room settee! She had a very happy satisfied smile on her face, as if she had accomplished the whole drive all by herself and got her human family home safe! Sweet smelling odors were emanating from the kitchen where plenty of delicacies were being prepared for the festival.

The evening brought with it a fresh batch of relatives and Lizzy had the time of her life sniffing everyone and ascertaining they were family! Soon the prayers got underway and small lamps of light were being arranged all over the house, hence it being known as the 'festival of lights'.

Lizzy diligently followed us everywhere that we went, to place the lit lamps. She tried smelling a few and probably got too close, because she jumped a few feet in the air and landed on her feet! She got so affronted that she growled and barked at the lamp, taking care not to get too close this time! She was dancing in front of the lamp, the way she does to a prey that she wants to threaten, jump over it with her front paws accompanied by barking! It's a wonder the lamp did not topple over!

When it got a little dark and all the houses on the street were bedecked with shining colored lights, the cracker bursts started! We ourselves did not like loud crackers. So we had bought only crackers which give off colored lights or which gyrate in endless circles on the ground. But there were a few bombs, courtesy my younger son, akhilesh!

We burst all of these outside the house on the side-walk, which opened into the house. The gate was left half open. The crackers were all collected inside the house, on the verandah, for the sake of safety. As we got them out one by one, Lizzy insisted on smelling each one. To our surprise, her reaction to only the bombs was violent! How did she smell it out that it was those which gave off the awful loud noise and not the others?!

The moment she smelt the bombs, she started jumping and barking in earnest! We had not put her on leash as is our wont. But now I tied the harness and held a firm grip on the harness while all the bursting was going on! She went berserk only when the bombs were being burst, barking endlessly, even after the noise had stopped! To all the other crackers, like the flower pot, the wheelies on the ground, her reaction was a lot more sedate. I left her loose once the bombs were done. Big mistake!

Akhilesh was lighting the circular wheelie on the ground. As the wick caught fire and it started rotating, Lizzy just sprang forward and tried to catch it by her jaws! To say we were caught by surprise was putting it mildly! It was a surreal experience! Here we were, all cackling and smiling and watching the wheelie swirl and suddenly there was a blur of brown and Lizzy was on top of it! As the sparks flew from the cracker, Lizzy jumped up and down and danced in between the crackling wheelie, all the while trying to grab the main body by her jaws!

"LIZZY!" I screamed, and ran forward to grab hold of her. "Come back here, you crazy dog!"

I yanked her harness and pulled her away, all the while taking care not to get singed by the sparks myself!

Lizzy came out and pranced around to get the sting off her scalded feet! She sat down licking her burns after that, all the while giving me side long glances, as if to say, "I couldn't help it. It was asking to be bitten!" But did she learn from these interludes?! Oh boy! She did not!

The hand held sparklers were her next target!

The moment the sparklers sprang to life, she made a grab at them! If we were not quick enough to turn away from her mouth, she would have probably burnt her tongue through and through! So celebrations were more of trying to avoid Lizzy getting singed by the cracker fire, than bursting the crackers! To be fair to Lizzy, she did try to snuff out the enemy!

Its one thing to hate noise and confront 'it' with single-minded devotion, to the extent of threatening to annihilate it! But its quite another, to be the cause of noise! See, that's the irony in the animal world. Any loud ear-shattering noise they produce themselves, is A-Okay!

Lizzy has an endearing habit of butting objects with her nose. Boxer dogs are known to do that. Because of their snub noses and stout faces, they butt objects, hence also the name BOXER!

Lizzy does not understand what is our objection to her playing and pushing the a noisy toy across the floor. She has a very injured look on her face when my husband clicks his tongue and tells her harshly to simple stop it! She sits in front of the toy, licking her lips, looking up at him questioningly!

"What did I do wrong? I am just playing! Please please, pretty please!" she begs.

If there is no rejoinder from any of us, she continues her 'game', pushing it across the floor with her nose, chasing it down with a healthy dose of loud barks and growls, butting it some more, pouncing on it like it were a prey, holding the edge with her teeth, and then dropping it just so that she can push it across the floor and start the whole process again! God forbid if the toy were to go underneath the living room settee, or behind one of the futons, or behind the refrigerator! Lizzy will then bark and bark at the disappearing tin, demanding that it come out and show itself, or else . . . . !

These barks are particularly loud and raucous, unlike her normal barks! These reach a pitch fit to wake up the dead and buried some million years ago! So the plight of the humans living with such a riotous disorderly noise, can only be described as being in zombie world, because all feeling in our ears has long since been snuffed out and our brains are actually mush!

How she can tolerate this horrible, nasty, ear numbing noise and revel in it, but get angry and agitated with the Diwali crackers, is anybody's guess! It certainly defies logic, but then Lizzy is a world all on her own!

If we are all sitting down watching TV or just relaxing, she insists we join her play with the tin toy! She picks it up by its edge and then trots over to us. She will then drop it in front of us and bark!

"Woof! Woof! C'mon, get up and play with me!" her invitation!

And she will not take 'no' for an answer! She continues to bark till one of us gets disgusted and throws the tin or kicks it away! Well in doggy world, that's solicitation! So as she chases the runaway tin, she looks back to make sure we are following her to keep the game alive!

"Woof! Hey! Pay attention here! You are not following me in chasing the 'ball'. That's not good sportsmanship!" she barks disapprovingly.

And then it starts again! The awful scratchy, screechy, banshee-like noise as the tin slides agonizingly on the floor from Lizzy's constant nose butts! Finally, one of the members of my family, not me, has to get up and hide the tin behind the sofa or in some other room! Lizzy takes that as an affront and thence starts loud almost continuous barks to bring back the 'victimized' tin! Of course, if we keep quiet and pay no attention to her, poor Lizzy stops and will retire sulking!

# (18)

## *A bow-wow company!*

Lizzy was around 2 yrs. old when we adopted Sandy!

Sandy was an abandoned dog from one of the local animal welfare agencies.

How anybody could abandon a 1 ½ yr old brown spotted gorgeous pure bred Dalmatian, was beyond me! We drove all the way to the animal welfare agency, some 15 km away from where we lived, picked up Sandy in our car, and drove back home with her. She was a thin waif like creature with all her luxurious skin hanging loose. She had a vicious cough and sat there in the car, trembling, with fear or fever, I am not sure which. But it took dedicated care and love and a whole lot of antibiotics and perseverance to get her back on road, fat and sturdy! Sandy co-operated beautifully! She never once snapped at us or nipped us during the entire process of getting settled in, even though I had to thrust the medicines right down her throat!

Lizzy greeted Sandy very suspiciously! Of course, Lizzy was suspicious of any 4-legged creature that took my attention! Sandy agreed to let Lizzy sniff her thoroughly but not get too pally initially! So it was face-off the first few days. But soon Sandy's tail did a lot of talking to Lizzy and since they were left alone together the whole day with my maid, Sandy was inseparable from Lizzy after the initial stand-offishness!

Lizzy was the alpha dog and she let Sandy know that in no uncertain terms! Lizzy dictated terms, when they played, where they played and how they played . . . . and Sandy played along! There was no clash of egos there! But if Lizzy got ahead of herself, Sandy being the bigger and bulkier dog, put her in her place!

Lizzy was used to having other dogs over. She knew her human owner had a crazy habit of sheltering dogs, all of which had stayed for a few days and then left. So probably in her doggie mind, Lizzy tolerated Sandy for the time being. But she was so independent that I wonder if she was actually glad for the company Sandy provided her when I was not there.

Much later, about 2 yrs. down the line, we adopted another abandoned dog from the same animal welfare agency, a black terrier cross, whom we named Rufus. He was a sweet friendly male dog, about half of Lizzy's size and therefore, about a third of Sandy's bulk!

One day . . . . the morning walk began pleasantly. The girls were high spirited as the weather was splendidly cool, with just the right amount of a nip in the air. Rufus kept irritating Lizzy biting her rump, dragging her leash, and generally being a mischief monger! The girls tolerated him, especially Lizzy, who earlier would go hammer and tongs at him!! Now she behaves like an elegant dowager towards an irksome teenager!

Everybody finished all their jobs and Lizzy and Sandy as usual got down to the business of chasing all the squirrels and cats and rats! So we returned back to go home. Halfway back, among the bushes, Sandy spied a white and brown cat! She was on it in a flash! Lizzy had not seen it at first! But she realized Sandy was on to something, when she heard her murderous growls! At that moment, Lizzy also saw or smelt the cat and she joined Sandy in giving chase!

All hell broke loose! There was mayhem all around! Sandy chasing cat, Lizzy chasing Sandy! Cat flying over the sidewalk, over the wall, across the large gutter! Sandy hurtling after cat! Lizzy flying behind Sandy and cat, now on the ground, now in space! Cat disappearing down the gutter! I heard a loud scream!

That was my voice, like some banshee in a hollywood movie! I was screaming at Lizzy not to jump, because I knew she would go to any lengths to catch the cat, even fly across a gutter!! She has been known to jump over rooftops, like James Bond, in hot pursuit of a cat! I have retrieved her from one of the hutments in the slum area after she jumped down one of the roofs along with the cat!

Thankfully, Sandy stopped and so did Lizzy! They cried like babies seeing the cat disappear! Lizzy howled in frustration, but she did not give chase! I think that moment was a defining moment in my life of 49 yrs.! My earlier life stopped and I was in my second life!! I could not bear to think what would have been my state of mind had my girls jumped across and gone in pursuit of the cat! The cat certainly used up 2 of its lives at that moment!

I collected my brood and we proceeded back on our walk to reach home.

In all this, Rufus, was seen carefully keeping his distance from the 2 big dogs, all the while yapping and growling for all he was worth! Being half of Lizzy's size and 1/3rd of Sandy's, he knew it was clearly unsafe to get in their way, especially when they looked so murderous!

The girls were back to normal, skipping along merrily! It was as if none of the cataclysmic events of the past 5 minutes had ever taken place! Two minutes later, I noticed blood on Lizzy's left hind foot! My heart literally skipped multiple beats! I stopped and bent down to examine her foot. Lizzy, poor girl, had sustained a huge gash, bone deep on the outer aspect of her left hind foot! It was bleeding tons and leaking blood everywhere on the sidewalk!

I held her foot and Lizzy helpfully licked me! She was feeling apologetic, saying sorry to me!

She must have hurt her foot while hurtling behind the cat helter-skelter and over all terrains! She did not wince, cry in pain, howl in agony, nothing, nada!! I mean what the hell was her limit of tolerance! Sandy in her place, would have howled the place down, limped, lifted her foot for me to caress and massage, the works! Lizzy actually pretended nothing had happened and it was all in a day's work! She walked and scampered like things were just fine! In fact, mid-way, she even found her favorite 'ball', a tender coconut to play with! And of all the days, today she had to find one of the really big ones . . . . and carry it all the way home to play with!!

By the time we reached home, she was bleeding profusely. Blood was splattered all over the road and on our parapet. The moment I reached home, I ran inside to clean her foot with dettol. I held her foot tightly, while I cleaned it thoroughly. I examined it then. It was a huge flap of skin off her left foot, over the toe, where there is hardly any depth of skin on the bone to begin with. The cut had run down to the subcutaneous tissue. She did not turn her face away, did not struggle, did not wince! This dog is just amazing! I applied medicine over it. She tried to lick it off. So I applied a firm pressure bandage over it, both to stop the bleed and to hold the medicine in. This Lizzy did not approve of!

She licked and licked and licked at it, till the darn 'pressure' bandage, became pressure-less! It loosened just a tad and the bleeding became copious!. By now, it must have started hurting because, Lizzy had a very injured look on her face and all the glitter in her eyes had turned dull with pain.

I packed it again. Lizzy decided to honor my second attempt. She just curled up on the floor and went off to sleep! I told my maid to keep a strict watch on her, in case she decides to lick. Licking dissolves the blood clot, thereby leading to fresh bleed. I was also to be informed in case she started whining or showing any untoward behavior.

I left for work after that. When I came back for lunch, the foot was swollen up but the bleeding had trickled to an ooze. The maid informed me that she had refused to get up from her position on the floor, the same place where I had left her, not even coming out for her bathroom break.

I cut the bandage, in case it was too tight, leading to venous stagnation. She came down to pee only then. I re-applied the medicine and put a light plaster over it, just to prevent her licks from disturbing the clot. I also started oral medication for her, an antibiotic and an anti-inflammatory.

I had my lunch sitting by her side, crooning to her. I slept with her for 10 minutes, on her bed, before leaving for work again. I knew that the medication would start working soon, and she would not feel any pain. She rested after that. But for the ensuing couple of hours, Lizzy quietly sat next to me, not her old self at all, but insisting on body contact with me. She slept peacefully, and came normally enough for her evening walk. But with Lizzy, one never knows if she has pain or not because she is stoic about it!

And so the saga continues. What pandemonium these 3 wreak on our household . . . . well that's another story!